GUS MATTAMMAL

A is for Average

Why California's Public Schools Struggle and How You Can Help

GONZO & PLAID PUBLISHING

1900 S NORFOLK ST • STE 350
SAN MATEO, CA 94403

First published by Gonzo and Plaid Publishing 2025

Gus Mattammal has no responsibility for the persistence or accuracy of URLs for external or third-party Internet Websites referred to in this publication and does not guarantee that any content on such Websites is, or will remain, accurate or appropriate.

Some names in stories told in this book have been changed for privacy. Narrative portions of this book are told to the best good-faith recollection of the author.

First edition

ISBN: 979-8-9986590-0-3

Cover art by Sara Patterson

This book was professionally typeset on Reedsy.
Find out more at reedsy.com

For every student who dreams of building a better life:
Education is the ultimate hand up

A little learning is a dang'rous thing
Drink deep, or taste not the Pierian spring

"An Essay on Criticism"

- Alexander Pope

Contents

Preface

Education is the ultimate hand up.

St. Louis, Summer 1984

I grew up in inner-city St. Louis, east of Grand Avenue, in one of the more violent parts of what was, and yet remains, one of the most violent cities in America. But the eighties were still the days of free-range parenting, and during summer vacation, every day had the same basic routine: I would read for a while in the morning, and then around nine I would get my bike, leave the house, and not return until suppertime. I was part of a small pack of neighborhood boys, and we would spend each day riding our bikes aimlessly around the neighborhood, making up games to play, climbing things of widely varying levels of appropriateness and safety, and just generally engaging in the kinds of foolishness that 12-year-old boys will engage in, if left to their own devices.

Early that summer, four of us boys were sitting in the shade, getting a well-deserved rest after a morning of aimless wandering, when one of the boys, Keith, started complaining about having to go to summer school for math. As I write this, almost exactly 40 years in the future, I have built a career and a multimillion-dollar business teaching math to kids, but even at age 12 I already knew I loved both learning and teaching, particularly teaching math.

So I offered to teach Keith. I told him I would be happy to spend the time with him and that I could quickly and easily teach him everything he would need to pass his summer class. But he refused, saying, "It doesn't matter how I do in this class."

That seemed to me a rather strange thing to say; after all, in those days you would be held back a grade if you failed a class, so the stakes seemed pretty high. But when I protested, Keith said something that I have never forgotten in all the years since. He said, "Listen Gus, you know you're the only one of us who's gonna make it in life anyway. It doesn't matter how I do in the class." And the other boys simply nodded along.

I was astonished. We were only 12. Yet the other boys had already given up on the idea that the future held any real promise for them. I had always assumed that other kids had a vision of the future similar to mine: that one day they would get out of this neighborhood and find a better place. My parents had instilled in me an unshakable belief that education was the ticket out, the ladder up that made achieving the American dream possible. In the end, my parents were mostly right; education was, indeed, my ticket out. Education, and a lot of luck.

The first way I got lucky was that I was naturally good at taking tests, so I scored well enough to qualify to be bused to the top public middle school in St. Louis: Classical Junior Academy (CJA). In order to get in, I had to take an IQ test. I didn't know what an IQ test was, nor that I was taking one; my mom just took me to a strange place one day and left me alone in a room with a woman who asked me a lot of bizarre and seemingly pointless questions. Fortunately, I scored well enough on the IQ test to qualify for CJA, and because of that I got a better education in middle school than I likely would have gotten at any other public middle school in the city.

Then came high school, and I got lucky again. All my neighborhood friends had to go to our local public high school, Roosevelt High. In 1986, the year I entered high school, Roosevelt had a graduation rate of approximately 25%, and 25 years later, when the graduation rate was *still* about 25%, the St. Louis Post Dispatch, St. Louis's primary newspaper, wrote "by nearly every yardstick, Roosevelt High School in St. Louis is the problem child in a district that is itself troubled." An entire generation of kids from my neighborhood— overwhelmingly low-income, Black, and disadvantaged—had been fed into that long-failing school.

But not me. I got lucky in a second way: my parents were excellent at long-term planning. My grandpa was a carpenter and a plumber, and his best friend was an electrician. On weekends over a couple years, my grandpa and his best friend hung out together and slowly remodeled our house for nothing more than the cost of the materials and an unlimited supply of Budweiser. They finished when I was in 7th grade, and my parents then rented out half our house to another family and started squirreling away the rent. That rent paid for me and my siblings to attend private high schools.

I attended St. Louis University High, an all-boys Jesuit high school. In addition to being 100% male, the student body was 99% Catholic, 98% white, and overwhelmingly from the affluent suburbs. For a skinny half-Asian kid from a rough part of town, it was a tough place to fit into. But I got a fantastic education there, and when the time came to apply to college, I got lucky in a third way: I had an excellent college counselor, Bonnie Vega. It was because of her that I applied to a distant college I'd never heard of: Pomona College, just east of Los Angeles.

The education I received at Pomona was absolutely amazing, as were the people I met there, many of whom I formed lifelong friendships with. Graduating from a college of that caliber put me on a path to an MBA from the Yale School of Management, and careers in television ad sales, consulting, operations, finance, and finally, private tutoring. The tutoring company I joined in 2003, Advantage Testing, has been called "the Institute for Advanced Study of tutoring services" by *The New Yorker*. After four years in our New York City office, I came back to California, to the Bay Area, to found Advantage Testing of Silicon Valley.

In the 18 years since, I have built a successful business in education that now extends to several states. I have personally educated over a thousand kids, from low-income youth through a partnership with Mission Graduates in San Francisco to kids whose parents are politicians, venture capitalists, and tech executives. I have just wrapped up a year as Chair of my local community council, and I have even run for Congress. I live in a little house with an ocean view with my wife, our border collie, and a couple thousand used science fiction books I hope to someday have time to read. In short, it has been a good life.

A life made possible by education.

Education is the ultimate hand up, the ladder that makes it possible to rise above whatever station you were born into and make something better of yourself. It is the engine of the American dream, and every time we fail to provide a child with a quality education, we all but hand down a life sentence of financial insecurity and the constant stress that goes along with it. When we fail kids *en masse*, sending generations of them into schools like Roosevelt High that function primarily as pit stops on the school-to-prison pipeline, we destroy the dreams of parents who hoped to provide a better life for their kids, rob kids of the foundations they need to succeed in an increasingly competitive world, and cripple entire communities. That is why it is so important that our public schools succeed in their educational mission.

But all too many of them don't.

In fact, an alarming fraction of our public schools in California struggle mightily. In the pages that follow, we will wrestle with the questions of why they struggle, what can be done about it, and how you (yes, *you!*) can help. It turns out that you are an indispensable part of the solution.

Let's talk about how.

Introduction

Meaning well is not the same as doing well.
- Unknown

* * *

In June of 2025, a story broke here in the Bay Area and went on to gain national coverage. First reported by *The Voice of San Francisco*, the San Francisco Unified School District (SFUSD) attempted to institute a new grading policy without notifying parents, and even tried to slip it in under the radar of the district's Board of Education (BOE).[1] As the article notes, there was exactly one reference to it "buried in a three-word phrase on the last page of a PowerPoint presentation embedded in the school board meeting's 25-page agenda."

Why did district leadership try to hide this new policy, rather than proudly declare it and explain its presumed benefits? After the story broke, the BOE asked for an explanation of the new policy, and in the public document, the response explains that the "key components of Equitable Grading Practices" are:

1. Providing students unlimited retakes.
2. Not including lateness, effort, or participation in a final grade.
3. The use of rubrics to standardize scoring.
4. Not including classwork or homework in the grade.
5. Basing the final grade 100% on summative assessments.

---

[1] If you are interested in the original article, it is available by accessing the chapter QR. I highly recommend it.

6. Using a minimum 50%, even for work not submitted, or a 0–4 scale.

Perhaps now you have a sense of why SFUSD leadership was not exactly eager to publicly disclose this policy before enacting it. *Effort* doesn't count toward your grade! If you know more than zero kids, think about them and ask yourself how much effort each of them would be likely to put into their classes if effort were not measured in some way or counted toward their grades. Homework, too, does not count! Ask yourself how much homework the kids you know would do if homework did not count toward their grades. Tests do count, but you can retake them multiple times, and under the Grading for Equity rubric, that 0–4 scale that is mentioned divides the percentages equally. Let me make the implications of that more visual for you:

	Traditional Cutoff	"Equity" Cutoff	The "Bar" under Grading for Equity
A (4.0)	90	80	🌑 Lower
B (3.0)	80	60	🌒 Lower
C (2.0)	70	40	🌓 Lower
D (1.0)	60	20	🌔 Lower
F (0.0)	‹60	‹20	🌕 Lower

In a traditional class, students are given scores ranging from zero to one hundred. An "A" reflects a grade of 90 or above, a "B" 80 or more but less than 90, a "C" 70 or more but less than 80, a "D" 60 or more but less than 70, and anything less than 60 an "F". However, proponents of grading for equity lower these thresholds to the point that even a student earning a 20 can pass with a D.

Moreover, the minimum grade for any assignment is a 50%, even if the student did not submit it at all. Teachers in equity grading districts across America now report students who do not even attend class and submit only a handful of assignments are passing their classes on the basis of that 50%

floor. This is plainly absurd.

The information provided to the BOE states that the San Leandro school district has already implemented the Grading for Equity rubric and has seen improvements in students' GPAs. I have no doubt at all about that! Under this framework, you can get a C without any measurable participation or effort, while submitting no assignments whatsoever and earning minimally competent scores on a handful of summative assessments (after multiple retakes). Yet, proponents of Grading for Equity loudly and forcefully insist that the policy absolutely does *not* "lower the bar." I leave it as an exercise for the reader to decide if you agree with that assessment.

But I didn't write this book to complain about one school district's profoundly misguided attempt to change its grading policy. More interesting is to ask questions like: what problem was this new policy trying to solve? How did we get to a place where a policy this misguided seemed like a good thing to do? Why are so many people ready to abandon a standard where an A stands for excellence and lower the bar to a place where *A is for Average*?

In this book, we'll address these issues as we tackle five different questions:

1. **Should we even have a public school system?** It may or may not surprise you to hear that, in fact, not everyone thinks we should. But the short answer is yes, and I'll explain why.
2. **How are California's public schools doing?** In a nutshell, pretty badly, if you're a kid from a low-income family. But, we will analyze this issue carefully, because only if we understand carefully how the system performs today can we have a productive discussion of how to improve it.
3. **How do we fix the public school system?** We'll explore several different ideas, some of which would be applied from the top down, across the entire system, and some of which would be applied from the bottom up, through experimentation and scaling.
4. **How do we make change happen?** Transformative change begins with leadership. We'll discuss the Superintendent of Public Instruction, the head of the public school system in California, and we'll talk about how

impactful that role could be if, *and only if*, we as voters choose the right person for the job.

5. **How can *you* help?** This question is something we will explore through-out the entire book. But, appropriately enough, it starts with educating yourself. In this book, I'll show you how. It is easier than you think! You only need two things: desire and guidance. A burning desire to help ensure that *all* our kids get a decent education is what you bring to the table. Guidance is what I will bring.

Before I do, though, I want to take a moment to address a bonus question: *Why do teachers do it?* Why do teachers show up to work every day in a system that, as we will see, is designed to produce mediocre performance for which they, the teachers, will very likely (and almost always wrongly) be blamed?

Clearly, the answer is not to get rich. Public school teachers are perhaps the most underpaid government employees. The answer also is not for the freedom of the job; in fact, to be a public school teacher is to be saddled with an enormous range of restrictions on what you can and cannot do. It is not for the external validation. So, why do it? Why would anyone want to be a teacher?

Over the last 22 years, I have built a multimillion-dollar business in education that is premised on the idea that education has the power to transform, to take people to levels of understanding that they may not have even thought they were capable of. The feeling that you get when you see a student achieve understanding in part because of something you said or did is amazing. It offers something that neither power nor money in and of themselves can ever provide: meaning.

And here's another reason: you get to work with kids. A plain and simple fact that tends to get lost in the strange and politically fraught national conversation we are having these days about birth rates and natalism and so forth is this: kids are *awesome*. By turns they can be inspiring, maddening, amusing, frustrating, sweet, and sassy. But the one thing they never are is boring. They are always interesting, and they are wired to want to learn. That makes teaching fundamentally... joyful. In a world that can at times feel so dark, the joy of teaching is a powerful source of light.

So, for those of you who are not educators yourselves, I've included a few tales from the trenches, stories of students I've worked with over the years. I hope these stories will illustrate for you education's transformative power and thereby give you even more of a sense of why it's so important that our public schools be as strong as possible. And if just one person reads those stories and is inspired to become a teacher, well, on that basis alone I will consider this book a success.

Finally, as you read this book, know that at the end of every chapter is a QR code that will take you to my website, www.AisforAvg.com; on the site, each chapter has its own page. These pages include a host of bonus content for those engaged with issues in public education, including links and footnotes referenced in the chapter, related or interesting material I have discovered since writing this book, and spreadsheets you can download and play around with!

* * *

Introduction QR code

We are what we repeatedly do.
Excellence, then, is not an act but a habit.
– Will Durant

I

Should we even have a public school system?

1

Smartness is the Wealth of Nations

An investment in knowledge always pays the best interest.
– Benjamin Franklin

* * *

Before we discuss how to improve our public school system, it's worth exploring why we even have universal public education. Universal public education is an extremely recent phenomenon, historically speaking. This begs the question, why make the massive societal investment in it? What good is it, really?

When I showed an early draft of this book to a friend, he asked, "Why is this chapter even here? Is there anyone out there actually arguing we shouldn't have public schools?" The answer is *yes*; there are plenty of folks who argue that. Many approach the issue from a free-market[2] or libertarian[3] perspective and generally advance three arguments:

---

[2] See chapter QR for one of the original papers arguing against government-run schools.

[3] See chapter QR for a link to an article in *Wired* that articulates pretty well the Libertarian case against public schools.

1. Anything government does, by necessity, runs poorly and at twice the cost that the free market does. Economist Milton Friedman long ago suggested that there was no justification for government-run schools any more than government-manufactured cars.
2. The existence of public schools puts the government in the position of imposing state-sanctioned narratives on the population, reducing diversity of thought and subjecting education to the shifting winds of politics.
3. Public schools are an infringement on civil liberty and parental choice, forcing families to participate in a system they may not support.

All three of these concerns are valid and will be addressed later in this book. For now, let us say that these issues are addressable in a *high-functioning* public school system and shift our focus to the arguments for having such a public school system.

There are generally five arguments for compulsory public education. First, education is the bedrock upon which our democracy rests. As James Madison, principal author of our Constitution, wrote, "A well-instructed people alone can be permanently a free people." In this view, democracy requires a certain baseline level of education to function properly, and universal public education ensures that we achieve that baseline.

Second, public education is an important step toward achieving the goal of equal opportunity for all. Education, after all, is a critical factor in social mobility. Research consistently links school quality to children's development, likelihood of graduating from college, and economic outcomes in adulthood.[4] That was certainly true in my case; I would never have gotten out of my rough neighborhood and gone on to live the life I have were it not for my great education, including the public middle school I attended. As the Urban Institute notes in their Upward Mobility Initiative:

---

[4] Take a look at the chapter QR for a link to the Upward Mobility Initiative. There is a wealth of interesting information on the relationship between school quality and social mobility.

School quality influences children's cognitive and social development. Lower-quality schools reduce children's chances of attending and succeeding at postsecondary institutions, negatively affecting their potential for economic success in adulthood.

As Californians, we should be especially mindful of this point, given how poorly our public schools are performing.

Third, public schools bring together a diverse group of students and, consequently, help to create a shared civic culture and sense of national identity. Robert Putnam, author of *Bowling Alone: The Collapse and Revival of American Community*, argues that a strong society creates two kinds of capital: bonding capital, which is the bonding between people of similar backgrounds, and bridging capital, which is the bonding between people of different backgrounds. In this view, to the extent our public schools provide bridging capital, they add something valuable that may be difficult to achieve at scale through other means.

Fourth, public schools form a part of the social safety net via their role as a hub of resources. For example, students and families receive disability services under the Individuals with Disabilities Education Act. Homeless students[5] are supported through wraparound services provided under McKinney–Vento protections. Students facing food insecurity are guaranteed two free meals per day through state and federal nutrition programs. Often schools provide mental health care on campus through school-based therapists, counselors, and social workers. Many schools provide additional resources in excess of that baseline as well. While there is certainly room for a robust discussion about whether public schools are truly the best vehicle for the delivery of these services and resources, the fact remains that hundreds of thousands of students do rely on the school system in this way.

Fifth, public education ensures the broadest possible development of a skilled workforce, which, in turn, makes America more competitive, espe-

---

[5] The California Department of Education estimates that 4% of California's public school students are homeless.

cially as the world continues to evolve from a manufacturing-based economy to a knowledge-based, services economy. As the Brookings Institution notes in its article "Twelve Facts About the Economics of Education," a person with a professional degree will experience one-fourth the level of unemployment and three times the weekly earnings of someone whose education level is less than a high school diploma. Similarly, a person with a bachelor's degree earns twice as much as and experiences half the unemployment of a high school dropout, on average.[6]

These are the main arguments for public education. Each one on its own has real merit, and collectively they make a compelling case. However, "democracy," "equality of opportunity," "civic culture," "safety nets," and "economic competitiveness" are all abstractions; they are almost certainly tangential to your actual day-to-day experience.

Consequently, in arguing that we should, in fact, have a well-functioning public school system, I want to take the fifth argument, about economic competitiveness, put it on steroids, and then tie it tightly to something more directly near and dear to you: your raw, naked self-interest.

You, dear reader, have the privilege of living in what is, in my (admittedly not very humble) opinion, the greatest country on Earth. And it's not just my opinion; it's clearly the opinion of a significant fraction of the world's population, who would jump at the chance to live here if they could. The American lifestyle you and I enjoy is, relative to what most of the rest of the world experiences, unambiguously awesome. And that lifestyle you and I enjoy depends crucially on one thing: smartness.

What do I mean by smartness? Here's how I define it:

SMARTNESS = ABILITY + EDUCATION

Smartness is crucial to your lifestyle because smartness leads to ideas, and ideas lead to technology. Technology then leads to business, and business

---

[6] See chapter QR for a link to *The Brookings Institution*: "Twelve Facts About the Economics of Education".

generates our national wealth. And that national wealth, here in the richest society in the history of the world, provides you and me with our American lifestyle.

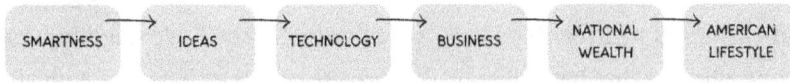

SMARTNESS → IDEAS → TECHNOLOGY → BUSINESS → NATIONAL WEALTH → AMERICAN LIFESTYLE

Take it from someone who went on exchange in high school to what was then the Soviet Union, and who has wandered through the slums of Mumbai, Havana, Cairo, and Nairobi: we have a great thing going here in America, and what keeps that great thing going is smartness. Smartness is the true wealth of nations, and as a country, we have only two ways to acquire it: either we produce it domestically, or we import it from abroad. Producing it domestically should be a primary function of a well-designed, well-functioning public school system.

Remember, *smartness = ability + education*. Most of the rest of this book will discuss education, so let us have a brief discussion about ability. By "ability" I mean raw intellectual talent, and it is something that has been extensively studied by social scientists around the world. Here are two key statements about ability[7] that reflect the general consensus of the social scientists who study it:

1. Ability is randomly distributed in the general population.
2. Ability is somewhere between 40–80% genetically determined, though environmental factors can impact its development and expression either positively or negatively.

To be a high-functioning society, we need people to play a lot of different roles, all of which have value. One of those roles is to be a person who

---

[7] See chapter QR to the editorial "Mainstream Science on Intelligence: An Editorial With 52 Signatories, History, and Bibliography". This editorial lists 25 statements considered mainstream within the field.

comes up with the ideas that lead to technology, business, wealth, and your American lifestyle. Those ideas will come primarily (though not *exclusively*) from people who have both a high degree of ability and a high degree of education. An analysis by *The Hamilton Project*, an economic policy initiative of The Brookings Institution found that almost three-fourths of high-quality patents are filed by inventors with a graduate degree.[8] We need to identify everyone who has that level of ability and make sure they have the opportunity to achieve that level of education. The more such people we have in America, the more "high-quality patents" we will produce: in 2020, for example, the United States produced about 30% of the world's high-quality patents, despite having only 4% of the world's population.[9] Nobel prizes tell a similar story: the U.S. has won 423 Nobel prizes, which is around 45% of all the Nobel prizes ever awarded.[10] The next closest country is the United Kingdom, at just 143 Nobels. Our ability as a country to produce and import enough smartness to outperform other countries in innovation leads directly, via the chain I showed you, to the maintenance of your American lifestyle.

Further, if ability is randomly distributed in the population, then it is imperative that we have a public school system that functions well *everywhere*, not just in a few lucky places. Partly that is out of a basic sense of fairness: every child should have access to a quality education. But it is also partly for the very basic self-interest we all have in ensuring that our school system can identify and develop all our best intellectual talent, which, by virtue of being randomly distributed, could appear anywhere.

The system's ability to develop that talent is key. A well-designed, high-functioning school system can take any student, whether that student is a student with intellectual disability or is a student of exceptional intellectual gifts, and develop that student to the best of their ability, while recognizing that "the best of their ability" is potentially radically different from student to student. By developing every student to the best of their ability, the system

---

[8] See chapter QR for a link to *The Hamilton Project* "Eleven facts about innovation and patents."

[9] See chapter QR for a link to a nice chart of patents by country in 2020.

[10] See chapter QR for a link to the *Wikipedia* page with Nobel prizes by country.

would ensure that we develop the maximum amount of smartness from our own population.

So, should we have a public school system? Yes, we should. But it needs to be both well-designed and well-functioning to be worth the enormous investment of resources it takes to have such a system at all. This begs the question: how well-designed and well-functioning is California's 130-billion-dollar-per-year school system? How good is it at producing smartness *everywhere*?

* * *

How *You* Can Help

The key to helping make our school system better is, appropriately enough, education. What we have to do is educate you about the current system. I will guide you in how to do that, and I promise it's not hard. I've educated over a thousand kids, primarily by providing guidance and periodic explanations of things. I'll do the same for you!

As we move through the book, and you begin to educate yourself about our school system, I will leave you with three levels of guidance: a basic level, that will give you the working knowledge of the system; an intermediate level, for those who want to dig a little deeper; and what I like to call the "Jedi level," for those who have an exceptional desire to push themselves and maximize their impact.

Let us begin!

The first step toward understanding the school system overall is to understand your own school district. It will be difficult for you to help the overall system if you do not first have a grasp of your own district. Here are some things you can do to start understanding your own district:

Basic level:

Search up your school district's website. For example, mine is "Cabrillo Unified." If you are not sure what your school district is, look up the name of your nearest public school. The individual school's website will always indicate somewhere which district the school belongs to.

Once on your district website, look up who the district Superintendent is. Often this information is contained in an "About Us" option. The Superintendent is the leader of your district. Who is this person? How long have they served in the role? What was their background before taking the job?

Change and improvement require supportive leadership at the top, and while everyone will say the right words, understanding who your Superintendent is and observing them in the role for a while will give you a sense of whether they follow up the right words with any meaningful actions.

Intermediate level:

Look up the different members of your school board. Who are they? What are their backgrounds? How long have they been serving on the board? You want to get a good sense of each of the people. Because most voters fail to pay sufficient to school board races, sometimes people serve on school boards for decades, preventing anyone with fresh ideas and perspectives from serving.

Join a group of folks from your school district who, like you, are passionate about education and want to get involved in helping improve our schools. You can use the "How *You* Can Help" ideas in this book to assist in organizing your activity as a group. You might have to do a little networking on social media or in local parent groups to find some like minded folks, but they are out there!

Jedi level:

Assemble a group of people who, like you, are passionate about education and want to see our school system improve. Organize a monthly meeting; you can use the content from this book for your agendas. Every group like this needs one person who is willing to do the work to organize the meetings and agendas. Be that person! That's Jedi level.

* * *

Chapter 1 QR code

A republican form of government, without intelligence in the people,
must be a tragedy.
– Horace Mann

2

Interlude: Mean Girls

When I train new tutors on my team, one thing I always tell them is that every student will come to them with both a family narrative and a personal narrative about who they are as learners and what their ability is. I teach my tutors that it is their job to (a) understand carefully and accurately what those narratives are, and (b) not buy into them. This story illustrates why.

Twenty years ago, I began SAT tutoring with a girl who was a junior at one of Manhattan's elite private high schools. As all of our students do, she took a baseline test prior to working with me, scoring in the high 500s on the verbal section and the low 400s on the math section, for an overall score just above 1,000. For context, that is an unremarkable verbal score paired with a fairly low math score, for a relatively low baseline overall, especially given the school she attended.

In an introductory call with the student's mother, she informed me that her daughter did not enjoy math and had always struggled with it, and that she was not a good test taker. Her mother closed by expressing skepticism that her daughter's score could really improve but said "everybody else is sending their kid to a tutor, so I guess we have to do it too."

Not long after that, her daughter showed up for her first lesson. We'll call her "Regina," because when she showed up at my office that first day, had it been Halloween I would have assumed she was dressing up as Regina George from *Mean Girls*. But this was just a regular day in January. I sighed inwardly and invited her to sit.

I began going through my brief get-to-know-you routine that I do in a first lesson when another girl walked by my open office door on the way to a meeting with one of my colleagues down the hall. Regina watched her go by and exclaimed: "Oh my god! I know her!"

I responded, "Regina, like thirty percent of your high school class comes here. You'll probably see someone you know every time you show up."

"Yeah, but," Regina said, leaning in and lowering her voice conspiratorially, "she's sixteen and she hasn't hooked up with *anyone* yet!"

At that point, I decided that get-to-know-you time was over and we began working.

Over the course of the first few lessons, I observed that Regina's math skills were indeed spotty, but I also noticed that when her guard was down, she showed flashes of an ability to learn math quite quickly. After surreptitiously testing this over a couple more lessons, I decided one day, without any warning, to take a chance.

"You know, Regina, I think I've got you figured out," I said.

Regina looked up from her work and narrowed her eyebrows. "Uhhh, yeah? What do you mean?"

I explained, "I see you've got the whole *Mean Girls* thing going on and, I have to say, you really have that persona nailed. It's impressive, really." I watched Regina stare silently at me before I continued, "But, the thing is, I can't help but notice that you also have a lot of engine under your intellectual hood, so I want to make you a deal: from now on, when you show up to my office, just leave all the *Mean Girls* stuff outside the door there, and while you're in here, I only want the engine under the hood. Just give me that."

Regina looked at me nervously, but I ultimately made her a promise that I would never out her, so long as she left the fake persona at the door and committed herself to achieving the score she so badly wanted on this test.

From that day forward, Regina started making rapid progress. She had committed so fully to the shallow, ditzy stereotype that both she and everyone around her eventually bought into it. High school is a strange time; there is a very clear social ecosystem with very clear roles, and even if you are lucky enough to choose your role (I was not, for the record), you still can easily end up in a kind of prison. But, a teacher can turn a classroom into a space where you are free to change your narrative. You don't have to be the kid who "isn't good at math." You don't have to be the kid who "isn't as smart as my other kid." (Parents say this sort of thing to me all the time.)

I offered Regina a chance to change her narrative, and she took it. When Regina sat for the SAT that June, her score went up 380 points, the majority of which was on the math side. I remember the number very specifically because when Regina's mom called me to give me the news, she said she and her husband had never imagined a 380-point increase would be possible for Regina. Then, her mother asked me, "What do you guys *do* there?"

I gave a polite non-answer to that question, because I could not, in the moment, think of a diplomatic way to say, *I didn't buy into your daughter's shtick, and neither should you.* But, I was thrilled that Regina had grown so much in confidence in her ability to do math, and I was glad to see her score reflect it. Even twenty years later, results like that never get old!

II

How are California's public schools doing?

3

A is for Average

Any policy is a success by sufficiently low standards and
a failure by sufficiently high standards.
- Thomas Sowell

* * *

How are our schools doing in California, generally? How is your school district doing, specifically?

Let me tell you a little bit about the school districts in my area. I live in a coastside town in the Bay Area called El Granada, but my main office is in a nearby city called Palo Alto, home of, among other things, Stanford University. El Granada and Palo Alto are separated by a low range of coastal mountains and Interstate 280. These two cities are only a few miles apart as the crow flies, but they're miles apart in educational outcomes.

In the Palo Alto Unified School District, where about 14% of students are Latino or Black, 88% of high school students are proficient in reading and 83% are proficient in math. Families in Palo Alto routinely send their kids to me and my team to prepare them for the project of applying to schools like Harvard, Stanford, and Berkeley.

Meanwhile, in the Cabrillo Unified School District, which includes my home town of El Granada, only 41% of high school students are proficient in reading and only 27% of students are proficient in math. In Cabrillo, where around half the kids are Latino or Black, often children of farmworkers, fishermen, or construction workers, the project is to get the kids into college at all, or, failing that, into a good vocation.[11] It is a completely different educational experience from what the kids in Palo Alto get.

Moreover, this disparity is not only evident when comparing *between* districts like Palo Alto and Cabrillo; it also exists *within* districts. For example, even in wealthy Palo Alto, where 70% of high school students receive As (i.e., where the average grade is effectively an A) fewer than half of Latino students meet standards for reading.

All across California, the story is the same. In Los Angeles, in the Beverly Hills Unified School District, 69% of students meet or exceed reading standards, including 55% of Black students and 67% of Latino students. However, just ten miles away, in the Compton Unified School District, only 43% of students meet or exceed reading standards, including just 36% of Black students and 44% of Latinos.[12]

For all California's talk of "equity," we've created a public school system where it really, really matters which school you go to. Go to one of the well-performing schools, and you are in a good place; you will probably get a decent education. But if you're not lucky enough to live in one of those districts, then you are likely to graduate without the reading and math skills to be successful in college or get a decent job in a knowledge-based industry, and if your district doesn't offer meaningful career technical education, then you also will not graduate with the skills necessary to get a decent job in a skilled trade either.

Is that fair?

I was raised to believe in fairness as equality of opportunity. It is fashionable these days to believe in fairness as something more like equality of outcome.

---

[11] The data on both Palo Alto Unified School District and Cabrillo Unified School District are sourced from the *U.S. World & News Report* and can be accessed in the chapter QR.

[12] District performance data is sourced from the California Department of Education's "Ed data" website and can be accessed in the chapter QR.

But, regardless of which definition of fairness you prefer, the one thing we should all be able to agree on is that California's public school system does not provide equality of *anything*.

Many people recognize how staggeringly unequal the system has become; that's why initiatives like Grading for Equity were created. Every time we measure the school system, whether through a traditional grading system, through standardized testing, or through observing which kids take more advanced classes, we see that the system is failing in its fundamental purpose of providing every child with a quality education. Fixing that failure is a hard problem to solve—a *really* hard problem to solve—so rather than deal with the long, hard, frustrating work of really trying to solve the problem, we settle for masking the problem with policies like "Grading for Equity."

I titled this book *A is for Average* not to signify a particular policy, but rather to signify a particular *mentality*. When traditional grading reveals a systemic failure, abolish traditional grading and implement Grading for Equity instead. When standardized test scores show systemic differences, get rid of standardized tests altogether (as the University of California did). When there are disparities in who qualifies for advanced classes, simply eliminate the advanced classes. Stop offering Algebra I to middle school students, as San Francisco Unified did, or get rid of Honors Biology, as Palo Alto Unified did earlier this year.[13] Problem solved! After all, if we lower the bar enough, the problem disappears.

The elimination of advanced classes is the most quintessential expression of the *A is for Average* mentality, because it looks at a disparity in opportunity (Black and Latino kids not qualifying for advanced classes as much as White and Asian kids do) and solves that disparity by *taking opportunities away* from the kids that have them.

Take enough opportunities away from kids and you will eventually achieve a form of equity. But, make no mistake: the *A is for Average* mentality is, at its core, an attitude of surrender to a two-tiered education system. It is a

---

[13] The chapter QR includes a *Palo Alto Daily Post* article about the (quite contentious) decision to drop Honors Biology.

surrender to the feeling that the problem is too hard to solve and that the shame of our collective failure to solve it is too hard to endure. Thus, we sweep the problem under the rug and tell ourselves we're doing it all in the name of "equity."

The reality is, all across California, we have a system that is failing to deliver on its fundamental purpose of providing every child a quality education. But what will really astonish you is the staggering amount of money we spend to fund that failing system.

The Price of Failure

As a California taxpayer, you pay a great deal of money to finance our school system, so it is worth having a good idea of what you're getting for your money.

The National Assessment of Educational Progress (NAEP) is often referred to as "the nation's report card". It is the gold standard for judging school system performance. In the 2019–2020 school year[14], this is how California stacked up against other states in the nation:

- 8th grade reading: 37th
- 8th grade math: 38th
- 4th grade reading: 40th
- 4th grade math: 44th

In the same school year, the National Center for Education Statistics ranked California 19th in terms of per-pupil funding (i.e., how much the state spends on public education, on average, per student).

If funding were the only driver of performance, we would expect California, with the 19th-best resource base to work with, to generally have around the

---

[14] The 2019–2020 school year was chosen because it is the most recent year for which both per-pupil funding data and NAEP scores both exist, and because it provides a snapshot just before COVID-19 hit.

19th-best results in reading and mathematics in the nation. Yet, we generally punch in around 40th.

Even more interesting, we can examine how well each state performs relative to its funding weight. Take a look at the 10 best-performing and 10 worst-performing states for 8th grade reading, for example, and their per-pupil funding ranks.

	Per-Pupil Funding	8th Grade Reading	Overperformance
Utah	50th	6th	44 places
Idaho	51st	10th	41 places
Indiana	38th	10th	28 places
Colorado	31st	6th	25 places
North Carolina	45th	22nd	23 places
Florida	44th	22nd	22 places
South Dakota	41st	22nd	19 places
Wisconsin	24th	6th	18 places
Montana	30th	13th	17 places
Ohio	22nd	6th	16 places

The best performers (2019–2020 school year).

	Per-Pupil Funding	8th Grade Reading	Underperformance
Pennsylvania	10th	17th	-7 places
Louisiana	34th	44th	-10 places
New Mexico	37th	49th	-12 places
California	19th	37th	-18 places
West Virginia	25th	45th	-20 places
Delaware	15th	36th	-21 places
Rhode Island	8th	30th	-22 places
Hawaii	14th	41st	-27 places
New York	1st	30th	-29 places
Alaska	7th	49th	-42 places
District of Columbia	2nd	51st	-49 places

The worst performers (2019–2020 school year).

As you can see, not many states manage to achieve less with more than California does.[15]

While we do not have access to 2024's per-pupil funding figures from NCES, we do have California's 2024 NAEP scores:

- 8th grade reading: 38th
- 8th grade math: 34th
- 4th grade reading: 37th
- 4th grade math: 40th

With the exception of 8th grade reading, which slipped a point, California has

---

[15] The chapter QR includes a link to interactive data, including the same analysis with cost-of-living adjustments. Factoring in cost-of-living, California ranks 34th in efficiency instead of 44th. It's still below average performance relative to other states!

climbed slightly in most domains since 2019, but the amount California spent to achieve those modest gains was 530 billion dollars over five years.[16]

As a point of comparison, consider the state of Mississippi. In 2019, Mississippi ranked 46th in per-pupil funding, yet they ranked 29th in 4th grade reading, already comfortably ahead of California despite spending one third less per student. But, the real shock is in how Mississippi improved between 2019 and today. In 2024, Mississippi ranked 7th in 4th grade reading. Seventh! People have called it the Mississippi Miracle. Mississippi did not dramatically change their spending on education, and yet they managed to climb 22 places in the rankings.[17] How did they manage this stunning success? We will learn the secret of their performance in Chapter 8, when we do a deep dive into reading.

For now, we have established that California's public school system is not delivering on its central mission of providing every child a quality education, and we have also established that California is not spending its resources efficiently. Fortunately, that means there is plenty of room to improve! We'll next look at a wide range of ideas for how.

* * *

How You Can Help

To best understand the issue of funding in public education, you should be educated about funding in your own local district.

Basic level:

Go to your school district's website. Somewhere on it is a link to what is

---

[16] These numbers are adjusted for inflation; if any of you are Kevin Drum fans, know that his soul can rest easy. See the chapter QR for a link to a spreadsheet with the source numbers.

[17] The chapter QR includes interactive data for Mississippi as well, including the same analysis with cost-of-living adjustments.

called the "Local Control and Accountability Plan" (LCAP). All school districts are required by law to post their LCAP somewhere on their website. Some districts have the link on the landing page; others put it in an "About Us" menu. Download the LCAP. Brace yourself, as it is a couple hundred pages long. The LCAP has a lot of useful information about the district's budget, how it plans to spend that budget, and why.

Start with the budget section. This should be at, or very close to, the beginning of the document. What is the total budget for the district? It will list where the money is coming from. What sources of funds are contributing to your district?

Next will come a section on goals. This section is tedious to read, so instead of trying to read it all, skim for the highlights. Don't get bogged down in the "why" and the "how it will be measured" details. Simply ascertain what your district hopes to accomplish.

After the goals section comes an expenditures section, where your district will list how it plans to spend its money. These expenditures will be listed by goal. Which goals get the most, or least, funding? What pleases, upsets, confuses, and surprises you about the budget? If you are part of a group, discuss your reactions.

If you are part of a group, an excellent activity is to divide the goals and analyze them more closely. Assign two people per goal and dig deeper:

- Why has the district decided to pursue this goal?
- How does the district plan to measure performance?
- Did this goal exist before? If so, how much progress, if any, has the district made in the last year?
- What progress towards the goal does the district hope to make this year?

Have the two-person teams work on this and then, at your next group meeting, have each team present their summary of the goal to the larger group. Depending on the size of your group and the number of district goals, it might take a couple of meetings; one goal per team will keep you rather occupied.

Intermediate level:

Complete the Basic level steps for a district that is *not* your district, but is interesting to you or your group for any particular reason. For example, I often like to compare Cabrillo Unified with Palo Alto Unified, because they are not very far apart geographically but are universes apart in resources and outcomes. As you do this, ask yourself, or lead a group discussion in, what the differences are between your district and the other district, and think about or discuss why those differences might be. Depending on your or your group's interests, you might do this for a few other districts as well.

After comparing to another district, and reviewing your own district's budget once again, ask yourself: if you could shift 5% of the budget around, which goal (or goals) would you take money *from*, and which goal (or goals) would you add money *to*? If you are part of a group, give this as a homework assignment and, at the next meeting, have everyone present what they decided and why.

Jedi level:

The LCAP is required to be updated every year and, as part of that process, the school district must hold at least one meeting that is open to the general public to facilitate community feedback on the proposed changes and updates. If you are solo, attend the meeting and give a public comment. If you are part of a group, organize your group to attend this meeting, and have each person give a public comment on the changes and updates. Someone needs to be the person who organizes everyone. Be that person! That is Jedi level.

I serve on our local community council (city council for an unincorporated area), so I have both given and listened to lots of public comments. Here are a few pro tips:

- Be respectful. You may well see something in the LCAP that makes you mad; for example, if you were in the Mountain View Whisman School District and noticed that the board had approved a $189,000 contract for

$1,200-per-hour guided meditations with a chakra healer[18], you would absolutely be right to be upset. But do not be the person who goes to a public meeting and yells; it accomplishes nothing except to increase the total amount of misery in the world.

· Type what you want to say ahead of time, and practice reading it aloud. Typically, you are only given two minutes to make your comment, and if many people show up, they may even limit it to one minute per person. Given that, the best thing to do is write what you want to say and practice reading it with a timer going.

· After you have practiced your two-minute version, decide which bits you would cut if you only had one minute to talk. Practice this version as well.

Go to the public meeting and give your thoughts calmly and forcefully. Demand accountability by being a model engaged citizen. That is also Jedi level!

* * *

---

[18] The chapter QR includes a *San Francisco Chronicle* article about this particular expenditure. It's so ridiculous that it's almost funny, except that it's an appalling waste of taxpayer money in a district where only 32% of Hispanic kids can read at grade level. So, it is *not* actually funny, unfortunately.

Chapter 3 QR code

The system was built to ensure that nothing ever changed.
– Margaret Atwood, The Handmaid's Tale

III

How do we fix the public school system?
Part A: On Schools and Teachers

4

School Funding

Every system is perfectly designed to achieve the results it achieves.
- Don Berwick, CEO of the Institute for Healthcare Improvement

* * *

Discussions about the performance of the public school system invariably at some point turn to the issue of funding. There are those who insist (often quite loudly) that the public school system would not be failing if we simply plowed more money into it. But, as I showed, other states accomplish far more with far less than California does. So more money, without any other substantive changes, cannot be the entire solution.

That said, there is one way in which more money actually *should* be part of the solution. In order to understand what that way is, you first must understand how California's public school system is funded today. To educate myself on this topic, I read a 200-page primer on how California's public school system is funded,[19] but don't worry – I'll condense it to a few paragraphs for you. As it turns out, there is a critical flaw in the system's design that must be fixed to see any real improvement. Only then can

---

[19] That it took 200 pages to explain how the school system is funded is the most California thing *ever*.

additional funds (which are also necessary) be effective.

Now, some may protest that they don't *want* to spend more money on California's public school system. I understand where that hesitation comes from, believe me, but in 1988 California voters passed Proposition 98, which requires that 40% of the General Fund (on a practical level, the state budget) *must* be spent on K–12 public schools and community colleges. It requires a two-thirds vote of both houses of the state legislature to temporarily suspend that requirement.

Thus, as our state's economy grows, and the state budget along with it, the education budget legally must also grow. That is, we are going to spend more money on the public school system *no matter what.* The only question on the table is whether we will spend that additional money feeding a system that is designed to fail or spend the money *fixing* the system. I assume, as taxpayers, most of us would prefer the latter.

So, having decided to fix the broken system of public school funding in California, let's first discuss its history and current state.

Proposition 13

H.L. Mencken once wrote, "For every complex problem, there is an answer that is clear, simple, and wrong." In any conversation about school funding in California, sooner or later someone will assert that Proposition 13 is the answer to why there is so much inequality in California's public schools. This answer is as clear and simple as it is mistaken.

Proposition 13 was passed by the voters in 1978, and it places a 1% hard cap on property taxes that are tied to the value of your property (such a tax is called an *ad valorem* tax). It further required that most new taxes be approved by the voters with a two-thirds majority before going into effect. Is this the cause of all our current problems?

First, a quick review of how property taxes work in California. When you receive your property tax bill, you will notice that it has three basic parts to it:

- **Part 1: the general levy.** This is the 1% tax on the value of your property, and it is the *only* part of your property tax bill that is limited by Proposition 13.
- **Part 2: payments on voter-approved bonds, including school bonds.** Every time the voters in a jurisdiction pass a bond measure that will be paid for by property taxes, a payment gets added to your property tax bill. There is no limit to how much voters may approve. Although Proposition 13 generally requires a two-thirds vote to pass bond measures, in 2000 Proposition 39 *lowered the threshold for local school bonds from two-thirds to 55%.*
- **Part 3: parcel taxes and special assessments.** These are flat fees added to your tax bill for specific purposes. For example, $10 might get added to your bill to pay to replace the sewer lines in your town. There is also no limit to the number of these that can be added to your bill, but Proposition 13 does require a two-thirds vote to pass them.

So, armed with the knowledge of how property taxes worked both before and after the passage of Proposition 13, let us examine whether Proposition 13 has made it unduly difficult to raise money for local public schools. In last year's election cycle (2024), we saw the following results:

	# on Ballot	# Passed	Success %
Local School Bonds (55% to pass)	266	204	77%
Statewide School Bonds (2/3 to pass)	1	1	100%
Local Parcel Taxes for Schools (2/3 to pass)	26	24	92%
TOTAL	293	229	78%

It is difficult to make the case that it is hard to raise money for schools when there were nearly 300 different school funding measures on the ballot, and the success rate was 78%.[20] School funding measures are just about the closest thing there is to a slam dunk in politics, just behind running for Congress as an incumbent.[21]

The problem with identifying Proposition 13 as the root cause of the school system's challenges is that the high-water mark for school quality in California was the 1960s. California started losing ground in the 1970s, and Proposition 13 was not passed until 1978. Let me show you a different graph. See if you can guess what it is a graph of, and I will tell you after you look at it:

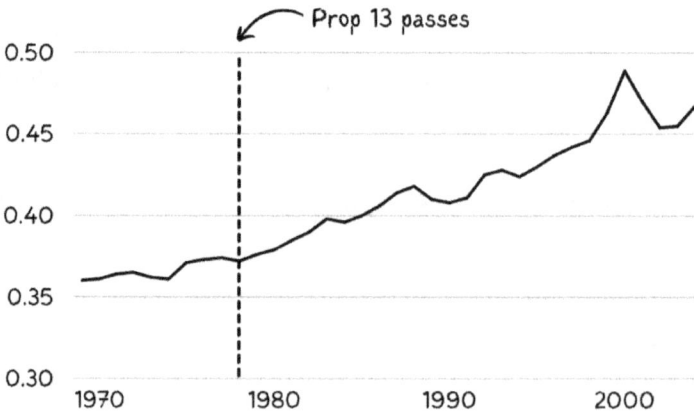

Based on the y-axis, can you tell what this is a graph of? This a graph of the Gini coefficient in California.[22] The Gini coefficient is a measure of economic inequality; the higher the number is, the more unequal the underlying society has become. The bumpy line is the Gini coefficient for California and the vertical dotted line marks the passage of Proposition 13.

As you can see from the graph, by 1978 California was already well on the

---

[20] The data for this analysis was sourced from *CaliforniaCityFinance.com* and is available in the chapter QR.

[21] Other than getting reelected to Congress. The success rate for *that* is around 95%.

[22] The underlying time series data is available in the chapter QR.

road to growing inequality. A funding scheme in which schools are financed primarily through property taxes is really only viable if property values are broadly similar in the vast majority of the state. In the fifties and sixties, that was probably close enough to being true. But, by the late sixties, property values were beginning to diverge. In 1968, the lawsuit *Serrano v. Priest* was filed in California, which asserted that embedded inequality in the state's property tax-driven school funding scheme violated the rights of students on equal protection grounds.

That case was contested at every level in the state court system, and it won at every level, including in 1976 in the California Supreme Court. The passage of Proposition 13 in 1978, by in effect accelerating the shift away from property taxes and toward income taxes as the primary strategy for funding schools, arguably helped make the system more compliant with the Court's ruling. Put another way, if we were still using the funding system we had pre-Proposition 13, but we had today's levels of wealth inequality and hyper-concentration of that wealth geographically, the school system would almost certainly be far *worse* off than it is.

For roughly 35 years after the passage of Proposition 13, California tried to achieve something remotely like equality in funding by using a system of revenue limits and funding for a thicket of specific programs. That system's complexity, opaqueness, and failure to deliver on its stated goal were, unfortunately, characteristic of so much of California's approach to governing. But California took a step in the right direction in 2013 with a complete redesign of the funding system for public schools: the Local Control Funding Formula.

The Local Control Funding Formula

The Local Control Funding Formula (LCFF) is the primary funding mechanism for California's public school system, and it's important to understand the basics of how it works. We'll use some simplifying assumptions so we can understand how it works intuitively.

Imagine that every child in California is holding a bucket labeled "base grant." When full, that bucket holds $10,000.[23] In keeping with *Serrano v. Priest*, every child's bucket is the same size.

First, local property taxes try to fill each child's bucket. If there are enough local property taxes to fill those buckets, then no assistance from the state is required. We call these *community-funded* or *Basic Aid* districts.[24] If a Basic Aid district can more than fill their children's buckets, they are entitled to retain the excess.[25]

There are only a few Basic Aid districts in California; most are in the Bay Area, with the remainder mostly along the coast. The vast majority of school districts in California are *LCFF-funded*, meaning they receive money from California's General Fund through the LCFF to finish filling up their children's buckets. When that's done, every child in California is then holding a full "base grant" bucket.

Then, there are two bonus rounds. Certain profiles of students (e.g., homeless, foster youth, low-income, or English language learners) are naturally going to be more challenging to teach, and it is reasonable to assume it will require more resources to teach them. For example, you may need to hire additional reading specialists or provide wraparound services and resources to support these students. Any student who has one or more of these characteristics qualifies their district for the bonus rounds, and the fraction of a district's students who qualify is called the *Unduplicated Pupil Percentage* (UPP). For example, if half of a district's students have one or more of the qualifying characteristics, that district's UPP is 50%.

For the first bonus round, the state hands each child a second, smaller bucket labeled a *supplemental grant*. This bucket is 20% of the size of the base grant bucket, which in our simplified example, is $2,000. However, unlike the

---

[23] In reality, this base grant is around $11,500, but it varies based on the student's grade.

[24] Even Basic Aid districts still receive some funding from the state for a few specific things such as special education.

[25] To me, it seems reasonable that property tax dollars should be retained in the communities from which those dollars come. Frankly, of all the challenges we face as a society, *people wanting to invest more in their kids* is pretty far down the list. But, you should decide for yourself whether you agree with me about that.

base grant bucket, which always gets filled to the top, the supplemental grant bucket is only filled according to the district's UPP. So, for our example district with a UPP of 50%, they will receive only 50% of the $2000 supplemental bonus: $1,000 per student. Only a district whose UPP is 100% would see their children's supplemental grant buckets filled to the top.

Finally, some districts are entitled to a second bonus round. In this round, every single child in a *qualifying* district receives a third bucket labeled *concentration grant*. This bucket can hold up to 65% of the base grant ($6,500 in our example). This is the critical point of failure in the LCFF. In order to qualify for concentration grants at all, the district's UPP must be more than 55%. For the districts that do qualify, only the amount *above* 55% is fulfilled. For example, a district with a UPP of 60% gets only 5% of the concentration grant buckets filled (60% - 55% = 5%).

Putting it all together, this is what the current LCFF model actually looks like for any given district. The x-axis is UPP and the y-axis is the per-student funding, assuming a base grant bucket of $10,000:

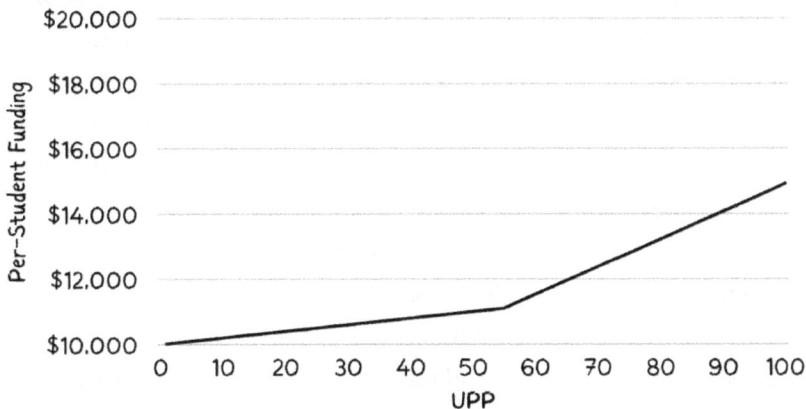

The design of the bonus rounds is where the California legislature got it wrong. Their design has two things going for it. First, it is well-intentioned. Their model does take into account that the higher the UPP, the more difficult a district's situation, and the more resources it will take to successfully educate

43

students. Second, it is mathematically simple. This model is only a couple straight lines, and it requires only basic algebra to understand.

Unfortunately, the LCFF suffers from one major flaw: it is completely untethered from the reality of teaching in an actual classroom. Visualize a classroom with 25 kids in it. At a UPP of 12%, you have three (12% of 25 = 3) challenging kids. A veteran teacher has a lot of tools available to deal with this. For example, they may pair the three challenging kids with the three most advanced kids in the class so that they receive peer support. The teacher may periodically assign an exercise to the class and, while they work on it, steal some one-on-one time with the challenging kids. The teacher may differentiate or scaffold the content in groups so each child works in their own area of growth. At a UPP of 12%, there are definitely workarounds.

Triple the UPP to 36%, and every workaround collapses. You now have nine challenging students. You almost certainly do not have enough advanced students to pair with them, and you cannot carve out sufficient one-on-one time to make a meaningful difference. At 36%, you face a dilemma familiar to teachers across the state: teach to the remaining, less challenging students and watch the challenging students fall ever further behind, or teach to the nine challenging students and slow the entire class to a crawl. If you do the former, the nine challenging students are almost certainly going to fail. If you do the latter, the remaining, less challenging students will likely never achieve what they otherwise could. This conflict arises at UPP levels well below the 55% threshold that triggers the second bonus round, and it is a conflict most California teachers must reckon with, because the average UPP percentage in California is well over 60%.

The problem with the LCFF's kinked-line model lies in its assumptions. It treats the UPP effect as linear, and it assumes the effect increases gradually at low UPP levels. Both of these assumptions are categorically incorrect: the effect is highly nonlinear, and it begins to exert influence much earlier than the current model predicts.

Why the Legislature designed the system in this way is open to speculation, but whatever the reason, its failure to capture the real shape of the UPP effect has been a profound disservice to millions of primarily low-income students. The result is a funding structure that leaves districts in an untenable position, expected to deliver equitable outcomes without the means to do so. However unintentional it may be, the system as currently designed is *built to fail*. That reality explains why California's educational outcomes remain so poor despite the billions of dollars the state allocates to its public schools each year, and despite the yeoman efforts of thousands of dedicated teachers and administrators across the state.

The first step toward a remedy is to recognize that the UPP effect is not linear at all; it follows a steeply sloping S-curve. There is, fortunately, a simple mathematical function that produces precisely that shape: the logistic function. The following comparison illustrates how funding schools based on this function diverges from the Legislature's current model:

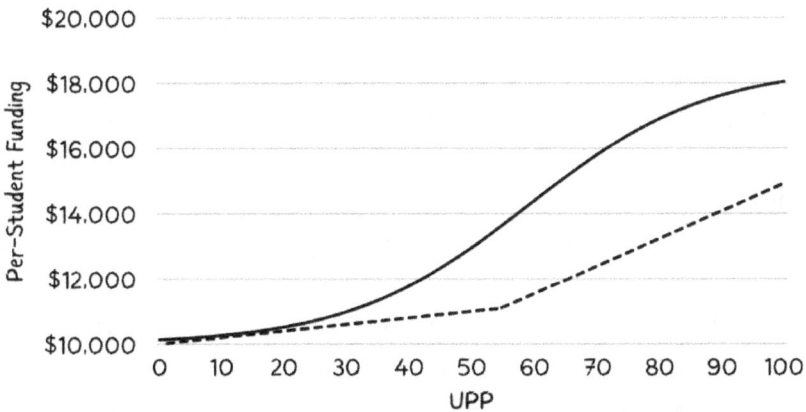

The dashed line is the current LCFF, and the solid curve is a more grounded proposal.[26] As you can see, my proposed model kicks in a lot faster and

---

[26] A picture of this graph that displays the detailed formula is viewable through the chapter QR. For the logistic function you choose two parameters that create the shape of the "S" curve; I use 0.59 and -7. This generates a proportion, which is then multiplied by $8,500 (the $2,000 maximum concentration grant plus the $6,500 maximum supplemental grant) and added to the base grant ($10,000 in this example), for the total per-student award.

far more steeply than the Legislature's model.[27] This makes it, in a word, *expensive*. The total cost of my proposal is approximately 20 billion dollars. But, remember this: as the budget grows, by law we are going to spend more money on education, *no matter what*. In fact, over the last ten years the education budget in California has grown at approximately 5% per year. At that rate, we will be spending an additional 20 billion dollars per year just three years from now, *no matter what*. As a taxpayer, do you want to keep funding a system that's designed to fail, or do you want to start funding a system that will produce better outcomes?

A few notes about this proposal:

1. All additional money that comes through this proposal would be used to hire new teachers or provide the facilities and supplies to equip those new teachers. The problem we are trying to solve here will only be solved one way: more bodies. More teachers to get the class sizes down. No other strategy will solve this problem.

2. This proposal should be phased in over time, similar to how the LCFF was phased in over several years. Any growth in the education budget beyond the rate of inflation should go toward funding this proposal, until the proposal is fully funded. Phasing in the proposal over time also allows districts time to find new teachers, set up space for them, etc.

3. Importantly, phasing in this proposal means we can fund this program *without raising taxes*. That is a particularly important aspect of the proposal for me, because we Californians are already very heavily taxed.

If we want to start funding a system that could actually succeed, we will need new leadership to pressure the legislature to enact this proposal. I encourage

---

[27] The chapter QR offers high-level model of this proposal by district. Each county has its own tab; within that tab, you can locate your district and view an approximate estimate of the additional funding it would receive under this plan. You can also download this model and adjust the two parameters of the logistic function to see how changes would affect both the total statewide cost and the allocation to individual districts. An instructional video on downloading and adjusting the model step-by-step is also available.

you to remember that when it comes time to vote.

This proposal is bold and hinges on spending the money to hire lots of new teachers. But we also have many teachers already plugging away in this system that is designed to fail. What can be done to support existing teachers? We'll talk about that in the next chapter.

* * *

How *You* Can Help

We have now had a very detailed discussion of the funding of our public school system. So, let's discuss how you can help on the financial side.

Basic level:

Use the chapter QR to go to my website. There, you will see the link to a spreadsheet entitled "Gus Mattammal's Supplemental/Concentration Grant Proposal Cost Analysis." Download that and look up your county, and then on your county tab, find your local district. Look up some of the basic financial information about your district:

- What is your district's UPP number? (Remember, this is the fraction of the students that are "challenging" in certain ways, and this number drives how much bonus money your district receives from the state.) How does it compare to other districts in your county?
- What is your Average Daily Attendance (ADA) number? This is how many students actually show up for school each day, on average. This number is crucial because it is effectively how many base grant buckets the district receives. How does this number compare to other districts in your county?
- What are your property taxes, and what is your property tax per ADA number? These numbers will give you a sense of how much funding comes out of your own community. How do these numbers compare to other districts in your county?

Intermediate level:

You be the policy wonk! On the first tab of the spreadsheet there are 2 cells, B12 and B13, that contain the parameters for the logistic function. Tweak them slightly, and observe how they change the total cost of the proposal (cell B19).

Parameter1, in cell B12, controls how steep the S curve is. A more negative number makes a steeper curve, which is therefore more expensive. Parameter2, in cell B13, controls how long it takes before the steep part of the S kicks in. A smaller decimal kicks in faster, which is therefore more expensive.

In addition, cell B5 offers a chance to increase the size of the base grant. Given that there are millions of students in California's public school system, a small increase to the base grant is very expensive. But you can play with that as well and see for yourself.

If you go to the second tab, titled "District Comparison Tool," you can pick your favorite districts and see how your tweaks impact those districts. Playing around with the model a little bit gives you a sense of what is possible and how straightforwardly we could amend the system to provide an enormous amount of much more effective support to our public schools.

Jedi level:

Search up "education committee California state assembly" and "education committee California state senate" and look for the "Members and staff" link. These are the folks who will or will not drive education reform in our Legislature. Write them a letter in which you argue that they should reform the way supplemental and concentration grants are calculated. Tell them this book has a straightforward proposal for how to do that in a meaningful way.

Most politicians assume (often correctly, unfortunately) that people do not pay attention to the details of policy. Defy that assumption. You would be amazed at what becomes possible when politicians realize people broadly are paying attention to something. Write a letter and organize other people to do the same. If you write the first one, you can let people riff off your draft so it's not as hard for them to come up with a letter themselves. Then you get much more bang for your letter-writing buck. That's Jedi level!

* * *

Chapter 4 QR code

Diagnosis is not the end, but the beginning of practice.
– Martin H. Fischer

5

Interlude: The Power of Teachers

I first met Abby in September of 2003, early in her 8th-grade year. She was my very first student with Advantage Testing. Abby had always struggled with math, and her most recent state assessment placed her between the 20th and 30th percentiles. Her parents wanted a tutor three times a week, primarily for math support, and secondarily for help across her other classes.

I and two colleagues were asked to a conduct trial lesson with Abby. A few days later, the founder called me and said, "Congratulations—Abby really liked you and wants to work with you going forward. Just one note: she said that after one hour with you, her brain hurt. You might want to throttle back a little in your lessons with her!"

From that point on, I worked with Abby across a range of subjects: reading, writing, study skills, executive functioning, and most intensively, math. Building both her foundational skills and her confidence was difficult—made more so by the fact that her 7th-grade math teacher had once made her stand in the corner and repeat out loud, "I am bad at math," over and over again.

By the end of 8th grade, Abby's grades had risen from mostly Bs to straight As, and her math percentile had climbed from the twenties to the upper forties. Her A in math placed her on a faster track for 9th grade, so her parents asked me to continue working with her. I did, throughout high school. She maintained straight As and excelled on the SAT. The summer before her senior year, I moved to the Bay Area to found Advantage Testing there, but we continued working together remotely. I helped her with her college applications, and I was thrilled when she was admitted to Stanford.

After I set up my office in Palo Alto, just down the street from Stanford, Abby stopped by from time to time, not because she needed tutoring, but because she wanted to visit. In 2011, when I married my wife, Jill, Abby was a flower girl in our wedding. I later attended her Stanford graduation and watched her leave to work in public health in Africa. Today, she manages a team in the healthcare practice of one of the Big Four accounting firms in New York. Though in my mind's eye she will forever be a shy 14-year-old girl convinced she'll never be good at math, in reality, she has become a confident, successful woman in a highly quantitative field. It is gratifying to see.

Such is the power of education and, in particular, the power of teachers. Teachers are human beings, like anyone else. Most show up each day, do their jobs well, and go home to their families. Some are uncommonly gifted at what they do. And some, like Abby's seventh-grade math teacher, truly belong in another profession.

It is especially damaging when one of those "wrong profession" teachers happens to teach math. Mathematics is uniquely cumulative: one weak link can break the chain entirely. But the reverse is also true. I mentioned earlier that I majored in physics and math, but I never intended to major in math at all. During my freshman year at Pomona, I took a class with Professor Shahriari. He was so remarkable that I simply kept taking his classes. By the time I had taken everything he offered, I needed only one more course to complete the major, so I did.

When I speak about education, I often ask audiences, "Who remembers having an excellent teacher?" and every hand goes up. Then I ask, "How many of you can still recall that teacher's name?" Again, every hand goes up. People can always remember an excellent teacher's name without hesitation, no matter how many years it's been, because excellent teaching leaves an indelible mark.

Let me leave you with this question: given the outsize impact that excellent teachers have on us, is there value in trying to recognize that impact in some way, beyond the fondness of our collective memories?

6

The Value of Teachers

The only people who are contented with a system of promotion by mere seniority are those who are contented with the triumph of mediocrity over excellence.
– Theodore Roosevelt

* * *

Imagine you were a recent college graduate considering two different career paths:

- **Career A:** Your compensation has some relationship to your job performance. If you do a better job, you get some combination of a bonus, a salary increase, and a promotion which, in aggregate, reflects (at least in theory) the value of your contribution.
- **Career B:** Your compensation has no relationship whatsoever to your job performance. If you are in your first year with the organization, you will make the same as everyone else who is a first-year, even if the quality of your work is higher. If you do better work than a person who has been with the organization for five years, that person will still make more money than you.

Which career path would you select, if these were your options? And which do you think would have an easier time attracting talent?

Most professions that require years of education and specialized training resemble Career A. Teaching in the public school system, however, resembles Career B. Yet it is common to encounter editorials lamenting the difficulty of recruiting and retaining teachers. These discussions almost always point to low pay as the primary culprit. Compensation certainly matters, but so does the fact that it is entirely disconnected from performance.

In *Work Rules*, Laszlo Bock, the former Chief People Officer of Google, describes what it takes to build a high-functioning organization. In a chapter titled "Pay Unfairly," he argues that most companies, in a misguided attempt to be "fair," design compensation systems that drive away their best people. Bock contends that fairness in pay does not mean everyone at the same job level earns roughly the same amount; rather, fairness means that pay is commensurate with contribution.

If we, as a society, want to attract more talented people into teaching, the issue is not only about raising the overall level of pay. It is also about changing the *relative* level of pay so that exceptional teachers are recognized with something more meaningful than a "Teacher of the Year" plaque and a brief speech at a staff meeting. Our current system assumes that teachers are uniquely immune to normal incentives and motivated solely by intrinsic rewards such as a love of children or a desire to make a difference. Teachers certainly possess those motivations, or no one would show up for work, but it is unrealistic to build an entire system on the assumption that other, ordinary incentives don't matter.

Another problem is that teachers' contracts rarely factor in whether they are teaching in a well-resourced district such as Palos Verdes, where few students are academically or socially challenged (its most recent UPP was 13.6%), or in a district such as Inglewood, only twenty miles away, where nearly all students face significant obstacles (UPP 89%). To choose the latter at equal pay would already require a very high level of intrinsic motivation, but pay at under-resourced districts is almost always *lower* than pay at better-resourced districts. Choosing to work in a fundamentally harder district for less money requires a level of intrinsic motivation bordering on the superhuman. A few teachers do make that choice, and they deserve our admiration and our gratitude, but most teachers understandably prefer to work in an environment where students arrive with greater support and stability.

Designing a differentiated pay system in public education is undeniably more complex than doing so in private industry. Public systems must safeguard against favoritism, arbitrariness, and abuse, especially within civil service structures that limit managerial discretion. Yet difficulty does not mean impossibility. There are already models within the public sector that demonstrate how differential compensation can be administered fairly. Police departments, for example, routinely offer promotions, pay incentives, and bonuses for officers who take on higher-risk assignments, earn specialized certifications, or serve in particularly challenging precincts. The same principle could apply to teaching if the state had the will to design such a system carefully and transparently.

Some districts have experimented with small, local incentive programs to attract teachers, but these efforts are typically ad hoc, limited in duration, and modest in funding. As a result, their impact has been minimal. The consequence is predictable: while the profession already struggles to recruit teachers in general, it is even more difficult to direct the most talented educators to the schools that need them most. A thoughtfully designed supplemental pay system would recognize individual effort and meaningfully incentivize the recruitment and retention of top talent in the schools that need it most.

One approach to achieve such a system is a statewide performance-related bonus pool. This system would serve two purposes: attracting new teachers when school funding reforms are implemented and directing top talent toward the districts that face the greatest challenges. To be clear, this approach would not reduce any teacher's paycheck; it would provide *additional* pay for every single teacher. But before presenting specific numbers, it is important to address two foundational questions in any performance-based system:

1. Who will teachers be compared to?
2. How will their performance be measured?

In considering how to form comparison groups of teachers, we must start with the observation that teaching conditions vary dramatically from district to district. In Coronado, students face far fewer academic or social challenges than students in San Ysidro. Piedmont differs significantly from Oakland. Comparing teacher performance across districts with such disparities is meaningless. High performance should be evaluated relative to the difficulty of the environment.

To address this, districts can be categorized by *degree of difficulty*, according to their UPP. Schools would be grouped into easiest 25%, middle 50%, and hardest 25%. Teachers would only be compared to peers in the same grade, subject, and difficulty category. This ensures that recognition and rewards reflect the challenges teachers face.

Turning to the question of how performance will be measured, the proposed model uses four metrics. The first is student test score improvement. Similar to how colleges consider standardized tests alongside many other measures, test scores would represent only one quarter of a teacher's total evaluation. In addition, rather than using absolute scores, the model focuses on year-to-year improvement relative to other schools in the same difficulty category. A school's percentile rank in improvement becomes its *test improvement score*.

The other three metrics capture recognition of outstanding teaching within the school community. Identifying top teachers is not difficult: students, parents, and colleagues locally know who the stars are. The challenge is capturing that local knowledge via a consistent, statewide process.

To accomplish this, at the end of the school year, each teacher would receive a <u>voluntary</u> form with three slots to nominate other teachers who excel, with no justification required. Each nomination would count as one point. Points would be totaled and divided by the school's average daily attendance to produce a per capita score, ensuring that school size does not confer an advantage. The percentile ranking of these per capita scores would then become the teacher's *teacher score*.

The same process would be applied to students and parents to generate a *student score* and a *parent score*. Each teacher then would have four percentile scores: test improvement, teacher, student, and parent. These four scores would simply be added, giving equal weight to each group. The total scores would then be divided into top 25%, middle 50%, and bottom 25%, with bonuses awarded accordingly.

Some may object, asking whether collecting input from teachers, students, and parents simply turns the process into a popularity contest. In practice, teacher popularity is overwhelmingly driven by *being good at the job*. Teachers who excel naturally gain recognition from their peers, students, and parents. While rare exceptions may exist—an ineffective teacher with extraordinary charisma—they are extreme outliers. For the vast majority, this system identifies top performers clearly, using a straightforward (and entirely voluntary) administrative process.

With the evaluation process established, the next question is what the actual bonuses would look like. Any plan must address two challenges simultaneously: attracting talented young teachers into the profession and ensuring that the best of that talent is directed to the districts that need it most. The following chart illustrates a simple award framework both by relative district difficulty and relative teacher performance.

	Difficulty Level: Bottom 25%	Difficulty Level: Middle 50%	Difficulty Level: Top 25%
Performance Level: Top 25%	$5,000	$15,000	$35,000
Performance Level: Middle 50%	$2,000	$6,000	$15,000
Performance Level: Bottom 25%	$1,000	$3,000	$7,000

With an estimated 319,000 teachers in California's public education system, this plan would cost approximately $2.8 billion, or about 2% of the projected

$130 billion state education budget for 2025–2026.[28] For just two cents of every education dollar, it is possible to fundamentally rethink incentives and compensation for teachers. A newly hired teacher in a struggling district currently earns roughly $65,000 per year. A $35,000 bonus for achieving a top 25% performance ranking would push that teacher's salary to $100,000, providing a powerful incentive to excel.

Some may wonder whether a top teacher's performance is truly worth that much more than a middle-level teacher's performance. This question has been studied extensively. A study by the Hoover Institution estimates that a class of twenty students taught for one year by a teacher in the 60th percentile, representing the middle 50% band, will increase each student's lifetime earnings by approximately $5,300. A class of twenty students taught for a year by a teacher in the 84th percentile, representing the top 25% band, will increase each student's lifetime earnings by about $20,000—almost four times the impact.[29]

It is also natural to ask whether teachers in more advantaged districts should also receive large multiples. After all, teachers in every district work hard. That is why all teachers receive a bonus under this model. But we have a crisis in our school system. Today, only 20% of Black 3rd graders in San Francisco can read at grade level; teachers performing here at a high level provide an invaluable service, both to their students and to society. Their compensation should reflect the *additional* value they contribute, relative to other teachers.

After all, it's only fair.

Recruiting and Retaining Good Teachers

Having made the case for funding a significant increase in the number of teachers in California and for a performance-based bonus system that incentivizes teachers to work in the most difficult districts, it is practical to

---

[28] The chapter QR includes a spreadsheet with this proposed model.

[29] The study is available in the chapter QR.

ask the question *where will all these new teachers come from?*

California already struggles with recruitment of teachers, and fixing that problem requires two things: better leadership and better data.

With regard to leadership, the responsibility for teacher recruitment, development, and retention is spread throughout the education system. The consequence of this distributed responsibility is that, with no single owner, the challenge of building and managing the teacher workforce effectively becomes a problem that everyone discusses, yet no one addresses decisively. The result is predictable: a system set up for failure.

Given its scale and scope, the California Department of Education should take the role of a lead agency in coordinating a systemwide strategy for teacher recruitment, development, and retention. Because these issues impact the higher education system, which is not within the purview of the CDE, the Department cannot assume sole responsibility for the issue. But it could take a lead agency role in bringing together the disparate players in the system and driving the development and implementation of a coherent, systemwide strategy. Of course, that would require energetic and assertive leadership at the top of the CDE, which we do not have currently and have not had in some time.

But we *can* have that kind of leadership, if we choose it.

With regard to data, even a cursory review of the data California collects helps one understand why California puts up such lackluster performance as an education system. Improvement requires a system of data collection, presentation, and analysis that is high-quality, comprehensive, and trans-parent. We do not have any of that today. The data is fragmented, spread across various systems, and is difficult to use because it is rarely granular enough and the reporting is highly inflexible.

For example, to build the valuation model for my proposal in Chapter 3, I researched the financial and student demographic data for all 900+ school districts in California. I can tell you from experience that in various places the data is missing, inaccurate, or out-of-date. In some places, numbers that should match do not, and in other places data is deliberately withheld.[30]

While the financial and student outcome data in California is concerning, the situation appears even more troubling when it comes to teacher recruitment, development, and retention. It is unclear that much meaningful data is collected, and what is collected is neither transparent nor easily accessible.

California has a unique advantage in its wealth of technology companies with world-class expertise in collecting, maintaining, and analyzing large datasets. An effective leader at the CDE could leverage this expertise by bringing in civic-minded representatives from the tech industry to help design a comprehensive, granular, and user-friendly data system. Such a system would provide enormous value, enabling education agencies, independent researchers, and the public (who, after all, are currently paying $130 billion per year for a system with shoddy data) to understand the system's performance and identify actionable paths for improvement.

With strong leadership and a robust data infrastructure, California could significantly enhance its capacity to recruit, develop, and retain talented educators. Implementing these improvements is essential if the state is ever to address the persistent two-tiered outcomes that the current education system produces.

Teacher Retirement

Implicit in the social contract with teachers, and with many other public servants, is the understanding that they will earn less in the public sector than they might in the private sector. In return, they receive far more robust and secure retirement benefits in the form of pensions. This is a reasonable social contract, but the details of the pension program matter greatly.

---

[30] Try looking up the performance of Black students at Pomona High in the Pomona Unified School District in LA County, for example. The information is listed as REDACTED in the underlying data table, and no reason is given as to why that is; if it's for statutory privacy-protection reasons, that should be stated. Though with 71 Black students, it's hard to see why that would be. Regardless, I think we can safely rule out *because the numbers are really amazing!* as an explanation.

For teachers, the pension system is generous, *provided* they remain in the profession for a long career. But is a long teaching career typical? Research conducted by Reason Foundation has examined this question for teachers in California, as well as several other states and yielded two key insights:

1. California's pension system is indeed generous for long-term teachers, as evidenced by relatively high retention rates compared with other states.[31]
2. Roughly 30% of all teachers leave the profession within five years.

The reasons for leaving vary. Some teachers decide to pursue other careers, others choose to focus on starting families, and some simply have a negative experience in schools. A study cited by *District Administration* identifies pressure, lack of administrative support, inadequate preparation, and low pay as common reasons teachers depart.[32] Whatever the cause, teachers who leave after only a few years are effectively shortchanged by the current defined benefit pension system, which heavily favors long-term service.

Given these realities, and the fact that many newer teachers cite low pay as a major factor in their decision to leave, a potential solution is to offer all new teachers a choice between two retirement options:

- **Option 1:** Receive a 10% increase on the locally negotiated base salary and contribute to a portable defined <u>contribution</u> pension system.[33] The teacher contribution would be 12% of salary, and the district would match an additional 10%.
- **Option 2:** Join the traditional defined benefit plan under the terms

---

[31] A chart from the Reason Foundation showing this result is available on the *A is For Average* website through the chapter QR code.

[32] The *District Administration* article is available in the chapter QR.

[33] If you want to know more about the difference between defined benefit and defined contribution retirement plans (which really is something worth knowing the basics of), then the chapter QR has a link to the Department of Labor, which has a good, brief explanation of the basics.

established in the local district contract.

Teachers who choose Option 1 would have a one-time opportunity, within the first five years, to convert to Option 2. After five years, the conversion window would close permanently.

This proposal has several advantages:

1. By citing low pay as a reason they are leaving, despite a pension plan that is definitely more generous than almost anything in the private sector, many teachers are indicating a preference to have more money now rather than more money later. This is a perfectly rational preference, so offering a plan like this that pays more money now will be attractive to potential teachers with that preference.

2. The current defined benefit system essentially leaves five-year teachers with little benefit from having invested five years of their lives in the system. Because this plan is portable and based on defined contributions, this plan ensures that five years of investment helping our kids still leaves teachers with a healthy contribution toward their future retirement, even if they decide to change careers.

3. The conversion option allows teachers who discover a long-term passion for the profession to take advantage of the back-weighted defined benefit system once they commit to a full career.

4. California currently faces substantial unfunded pension liabilities. Teachers and other public servants make life decisions based on the expectation that promised funds will be available, yet the state has no concrete plan to cover these obligations. Shifting new teachers to a defined contribution plan ensures their retirement funds exist and helps protect legacy teachers by reducing additional strain on the defined benefit system.

Solving California's two-tiered outcome problem will require hiring many more teachers. *People*, in other words, are the only solution. Technology can provide some support at the margins, but the teaching workforce simply must be expanded. Achieving this at scale will demand stronger leadership at the Department of Education and fresh approaches to system design. With improved incentives through a robust performance-based compensation plan, better leadership and comprehensive data to guide recruitment, and expanded retirement options, it will be possible, over time, to meet the demand for new teachers.

What is required immediately, however, is leadership capable of driving these initiatives and pressuring the legislature and the governor to implement necessary reforms. Without such leadership, recruiting and retaining the teachers California needs will remain impossible, and the two-tiered outcomes will persist. California's children deserve better than that.

* * *

How *You* Can Help

There are plenty of ways you can be a positive force in teachers' lives.

Basic level:

If you have more time than money, write a thank-you card or send a thank-you email to a teacher you have some connection to, perhaps because they teach your child or perhaps because they teach a friend's child. If you hear about something good or nice that a teacher did, do a short post on your social media of choice.

In this book, I necessarily highlight places where the system falls short, because our aim is to improve it, but many good things do happen in our schools every day, and it is worth highlighting the good even as we work to improve where needed.

If you have more money than time, go on to donorschoose.org and look up some projects and classrooms in your area that you can help fund.[34]

---

[34] A link to donorschoose.org is available in the chapter QR.

Donorschoose is a great organization, and you can help a lot of local classrooms that need supplies and equipment.

Intermediate level:

If you are solo, look beyond your immediate area on Donorschoose and find a high-need school to fund some projects or classrooms in. The website has an interactive map, and the map color-codes schools based on the level of need of their students.

If you are part of a group, organize a group game night where people compete for money in your game(s) of choice. Toward the end of the evening, everyone takes their winnings and goes on Donorschoose to fund some projects. Fund projects both in your own neighborhood and in some high-need schools outside your neighborhood. You can enjoy the thrill of competition and the satisfaction of supporting kids and teachers!

If you can, organize a group of people and assign each person to find one local restaurant who is willing to partner with you to donate food for the staff at a local school. It only takes 9–10 people to be able to provide a once-a-month experience for the staff at the school, and then each person and their restaurant partner only has to do it once per school year.

Jedi level:

If you have a broad professional network, network with the leadership of one of your local public schools and offer to be a resource they can call when they are looking to source a particular set of skills. Often teachers would love to have someone guest speak on a topic; for instance, the Biology teacher might like to have someone in Biotech come speak, but she doesn't know someone in the field personally. You can be one of the school's go-to people for sourcing talent or making connections.

One of my favorite movies of all time is *The Shawshank Redemption*, and in the movie Andy Dufresne (played by Tim Robbins) approaches Red (played by Morgan Freeman) and says, "I understand you're a man who knows how to get things." Be the person that the school calls when they need to get something or someone and don't know how. Be like Morgan Freeman! That's *definitely* Jedi level.

* * *

Chapter 6 QR code

The mediocre teacher tells.
The good teacher explains.
The superior teacher demonstrates.
The great teacher inspires.
– William Arthur Ward

IV

How do we fix the public school system?
Part B: On Curriculum

7

Interlude: A Pound of Cure

Years ago, a Nicaraguan woman came to the United States as a refugee with her young son, Jeb. During Jeb's early childhood, he and his mom moved constantly, from one state to another, never staying long enough in any one place for Jeb to find stability in any school he attended. Teachers refer to this as fragmented education.

Consequently, Jeb struggled to gain a rudimentary understanding of the English language and never learned how to read. By high school, his mother's situation had turned desperate, and she became trapped in an abusive relationship. It was during this time that the gaps caused by years of interrupted education were being noticed by school officials. His difficulty in language and literacy was labeled as a developmental disability. He was placed in special education, not because of an innate developmental issue, but because the system failed to see the whole story behind his struggle.

The combination of domestic violence at home and a discouraging experience in the special education system eventually drove Jeb to drop out of high school and live on the streets. He remained on the streets until he was 21, when he stumbled across Job Corps, a federal job training program for young adults. Through Job Corps, Jeb enrolled and trained in culinary arts and, for the first time, he discovered a sense of focus and purpose. Jeb, determined to rebuild his life, threw himself into his studies, completing the coursework to earn his high school diploma. Consequently, his success allowed him to transfer to the Bay Area for advanced training, an opportunity that allowed him to refine his skills and work toward becoming a professional chef.

Once Jeb arrived in the Bay Area, surrounded by peers who were in advanced training, he quickly realized that many of them were more educated and articulate than he was. Jeb saw what he had missed and decided to pursue higher education. Determined to move forward, Jeb enrolled at the City College of San Francisco.

At City College, he focused on rebuilding the basic academic skills that he hadn't had the chance to truly develop. It was around this time that he came onto my radar. He told me he hoped to apply to graduate school someday, which would mean taking the GRE, a test requiring a strong foundation of math through Algebra II, a broad vocabulary, and advanced reading comprehension. But when we gave him a baseline assessment, the results were disconcerting. His scores were extremely low.

I paired Jeb with two tutors, one for math and one for verbal skills. After their first meetings, both tutors called me, sounding discouraged. The math tutor explained to me that "Jeb's math skills are basically 2nd-grade level." Afterward, the verbal tutor called me and said, "Jeb can read individual words, but he extracts very little meaning from anything he reads. If we're going to do this, I'll have to teach him how to read from the ground up."

I called Jeb into my office, and we had a long, honest conversation. I told him that we were willing to help him, but that if he truly wanted to achieve his goal (taking the GRE and applying to graduate school), we would need at least one to two years to rebuild his foundational skills before even starting test preparation, followed by another six to eight months of focused prep.

To his credit, Jeb did not hesitate. He agreed immediately to that plan. Over the next two years, my team worked with him pro bono, during which time he blossomed at City College and then transferred to UC Berkeley. He completed a bachelor's degree and wrote his thesis on the school-to-prison pipeline. After graduation, he returned to Job Corps, managing several centers and mentoring young adults who, like him, were searching for a second chance.

We continued working with Jeb through GRE prep, and his eventual scores were nothing short of extraordinary, given where he had started. My team guided him through the application process, and I personally worked with him on interview preparation. When the dust settled, Jeb was accepted to the Harvard Kennedy School of Government with a two-year, full-ride scholarship. His goal: to study how public policy can dismantle the barriers that prevent so many people like him from succeeding.

Over the past twenty-two years, I have had the privilege of working with many remarkable young men and women through our various pro bono programs, but Jeb's story remains one of the most memorable. I share it because it illustrates the possibilities and the limitations of repairing a reading deficit.

When Jeb came to us, he was significantly behind on reading, and fixing that gap of knowledge required roughly 150 hours of individualized instruction over nearly two years—150 hours with one of the most gifted verbal instructors in America. For an average teacher, the process would take even longer. You may have heard the expression, "An ounce of prevention is worth a pound of cure." For every student who graduates from our school system far behind in reading, there is no shortcut. The only effective solution is a pound of cure: hundreds of hours of one-on-one intervention. That is the price for every child we graduate without the reading skills necessary to succeed.

8

Reading is Fundamentalism

Fanaticism comes from any form of chosen blindness accompanying the pursuit of a single dogma.
– John Berger

* * *

As I have argued, flaws in funding design contribute to the poor performance that characterizes much of California's public school system, and the lack of connection between compensation and performance makes it difficult to recruit and retain teachers. But equally important is the curriculum: what exactly are we teaching students, and does it truly prepare them for success?

Over the years, I have prepared many students for standardized tests. Whenever I begin working with a new student, I always start with reading. Reading appears on every standardized test at every level, and even when a student tackles a math problem, the first step is to read the problem and comprehend it. Reading is the most fundamental academic skill.

California, however, has done a remarkably poor job teaching children to read over the last twenty-five years. The most recent NAEP scores ranked California 38th in 8th grade reading and 37th in 4th grade reading. This raises a critical question: why is California so ineffective at teaching reading?

The answer is, in part, surprisingly simple. California deliberately teaches children to read using methods that cognitive science debunked long ago.

At this point, you are likely wondering *why would we do that?* Whenever you find yourself asking this question, there is a good chance that the answer is one or both of the following reasons:

1. Politics
2. Money

In California's case, it is both.

The Science of Reading

Decades of research have shown that how we teach children to read has profound consequences for their academic success. Evidence clearly favors methods that teach students to decode words systematically, rather than relying on guessing from context or pictures. Yet, many schools continue to use approaches that ignore this evidence, and understanding why requires looking at both historical choices and the incentives that shaped them. The following summary highlights the key developments most relevant to how reading instruction evolved in California.[35]

1. The old-fashioned method of teaching children to read—teaching them to sound out words and using phonics drills—is, empirically, extremely effective.
2. A woman named Marie Clay developed an alternative approach. Instead of teaching students to decode words, her method encourages them to guess words based on context, pictures, or other clues. This approach spread widely across the United States and much of the developed world.
3. By the late 1990s, cognitive science had thoroughly debunked Clay's

---

[35] For the full story on how California came to adopt this non-scientific approach known as *balanced literacy*, I strongly recommend the podcast *Sold a Story.* A link to the podcast is available in the chapter QR.

method, showing it to be substantially less effective than the phonics-based approach, which became known as the *science of reading.*

4. In 2002, President George W. Bush promoted the science of reading through the No Child Left Behind Act. This sparked a political backlash. Many teachers rejected the initiative not because of the science itself but because it was associated with Bush.[36]

5. By the 2000s, consultants and companies had built an entire ecosystem around Clay's approach. They had a financial interest in maintaining the status quo and resisting the adoption of the science of reading.

Politics is evident in point (4) and *money* in point (5). California could have adopted a science-based approach to teaching reading more than two decades ago, but these factors prevented it. The result is that an entire generation of children were taught to read in a substandard manner. The impact of that hits low-income students the hardest, as their families are less likely to have the time or resources to teach their kids how to read themselves or to send them to my team to rectify the situation.

As this book is going to print, California has, after quite a bit of struggle, managed to get a bill through the legislature that promotes, but does not *require*, the science of reading throughout the state.[37] In previous years, such bills have always died. But this year, the politics around the issue may have changed enough to make some progress, and the changing politics is driven by one state's performance: Mississippi.

In 2013, Mississippi passed the Literacy-Based Promotion Act (LBPA), committing fully to the science of reading. In the subsequent years, Mississippi's NAEP 4th grade reading scores improved dramatically.

---

[36] As one teacher in *Sold a Story* admitted, "I wasn't going to do any of that. And, you know, I wasn't necessarily rejecting the curriculum as much as I was rejecting Bush."

[37] This in a state that has absolutely no problem mandating things for the school system. For instance, they mandated financial literacy, which I wholeheartedly support. They mandated ethnic studies, which we'll talk about shortly. But when it comes to reading, the most foundational skill, the legislature *still* couldn't muster the courage to mandate the approach we know works. It's just sad.

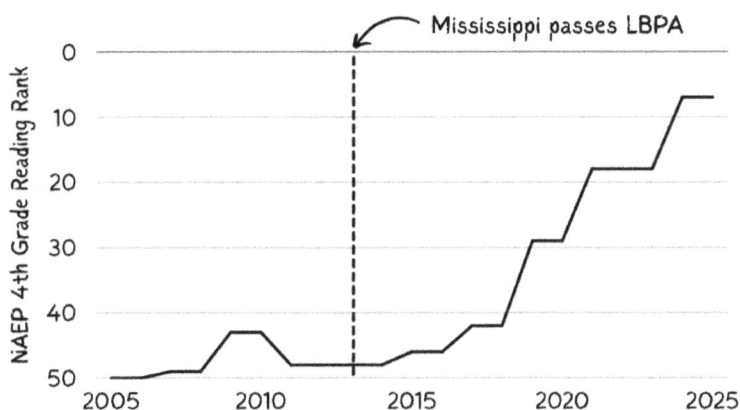

Under the science of reading, Mississippi went from 48th in the nation to 7th in just 12 years! Many have dubbed this the *Mississippi Miracle*. On the one hand, it seems like a misnomer to call a science-based approach a "miracle"; on the other hand, given that we still do not have a law comparable to Mississippi's here in California, it perhaps *is* a miracle that the science overcame the politics there.

In the absence of leadership from the state legislature on this issue, one obvious thing to do is to advocate in your school district for a reading curriculum that uses the science of reading and that dispenses entirely with the whole language or balanced literacy approach descended from Marie Clay; that approach needs to be taken out, root and branch.

In the podcast *Sold a Story*, one proponent of balanced literacy went so far as to state "If a reader says 'pony' for 'horse,' because of information from the pictures, that tells the teacher that the reader is using meaning information from the pictures. His response is partially correct, but the teacher needs to guide him to stop and work for accuracy."

I'm sorry, but if a student reads the word "HORSE" as the word "PONY," and you describe that, from a reading perspective, as *partially correct*, you are deep into the *A is for Average* mindset. If the goal is to teach students to *read*, then there is absolutely *nothing* correct about that response.

It is also worth emphasizing that teachers use Clay's methodology, in part, because it is how they themselves have been taught to teach reading. The politics and money that coalesced around what I would describe as Marie Clay's "balanced nonsense" approach have created an entire ecosystem of teacher's colleges and consultant-driven training programs that pushes teachers to use that methodology.

So, rather than wait for the state legislature to get around to putting our kids before their own political incentives and pass a statewide bill that actually mandates using the science of reading, I urge you to be a force pushing your local school district to adopt a science of reading curriculum, if it has not already. See the "How you can help" section at the end of this chapter for some specific ideas of how to get engaged.

Skills vs. Content

A second way in which we miss an opportunity to shape stronger readers is that we focus too early with kids on skills rather than on content. For a very good and very digestible discussion of this issue, I strongly recommend Natalie Wexler's *The Knowledge Gap*.

Wexler's central point is simple but profound: broad background knowledge is essential for reading comprehension. "Comprehension skills," without that foundation, are a thin reed to cling to. To see why, try reading the following 100-word passage, and imagine you're a student taking a standardized test, about to be asked, "What is the main idea of this passage?"

The Yang–Mills theory, proposed in 1954 by Chen-Ning Yang and Robert Mills, revolutionized modern physics by extending the principle of gauge invariance beyond the abelian case of electromagnetism to more complex, non-commuting symmetry groups. This bold generalization introduced self-interacting gauge fields, forming the mathematical foundation for the later development of the Standard Model. Though initially abstract, the Yang–Mills framework ultimately explained the behavior of the strong and weak nuclear forces through the exchange of gluons and W and Z bosons. By uniting symmetry, geometry, and physical law, the theorem transformed both theoretical and experimental physics, revealing that the universe's deepest interactions arise from the elegant structure of internal symmetries.

Having read that piece, how confident are you that you could correctly identify the main idea? If you are reading this book, there is a fair chance that you have a higher-than-average level of education, and you are obviously someone who knows how to read. This passage, generated by ChatGPT, describes the development of the Yang-Mills Theory, which I promise is actually an interesting topic, provided you have some background knowledge about quantum mechanics and the Standard Model of particle physics.[38]

However, if you do not have that background knowledge, then even answering a basic question like "What is the main idea of this passage?" is likely daunting. But, try this exercise again, still thinking about "What is the main idea?" but with a different passage:

In 2004, Mean Girls extended the teen comedy genre by exploring complex social hierarchies, selecting Regina George as the archetype to represent manipulative social dominance in high school. Regina's control over the group is challenged when Cady Heron rises in popularity, threatening the established balance. Regina's response, such as her backhanded compliments and social sabotage, can be explained by social comparison theory, which evaluates self-worth through comparison to others. Regina knew this dynamic well, having perfected it in her rise to power, but her tactics revealed the "unrealistic standards" of high school social life, exposing the fragility of her reign.

Are you more confident about the main idea of this passage? The answer is likely *yes*. But why? After all, this passage is identical in length and structure to the Yang-Mills passage (I know, because I instructed ChatGPT to write it that way). The difference is that you have far more relevant background knowledge to help you make sense of it. There is a good chance you have seen

---

[38] The *Wikipedia* article for Yang-Mills Theory is included in the chapter QR.

Mean Girls and are familiar with the characters and basic plot. But, even if you have not, you probably experienced "manipulative social dominance" in high school yourself, either on the giving end (my wife, captain of the cheerleading squad)[39] or the receiving end (me, a skinny half-Asian kid who liked math and physics).

Having a general content foundation is key. It is much easier to provide such a foundation when children are younger. As an adult, you may have noticed that learning new things takes more effort and occurs more slowly than it did in childhood. Children, by contrast, are like sponges, absorbing new information with minimal effort. Our current approach to education wastes this critical window. Schools often focus on teaching skills as the primary activity, while content is treated as secondary, rather than providing a broad knowledge base early on.

Almost the entire school system in California follows this approach. The difference between higher-income children and lower-income children, who are overwhelmingly Black and Latino, is that higher-income children gain exposure to content outside of school. They experience more language input because their parents can devote time to reading and conversation. Estimates of the "word gap," the difference in the number of words lower-income children have been exposed to by kindergarten compared to higher-income children, range from 3 million to 30 million words. Even at the low-end estimate, this equates to roughly 2,000 words *per day*.[40]

Higher-income families also have access to enrichment opportunities outside of school, including tutoring. My team and I frequently work with parents concerned about their child's reading, writing, or math skills. We start with a brief conversation with the child to identify a content area that genuinely interests them. Once we know what excites the child, we integrate reading, writing, or math instruction into that content area. The school system, by contrast, focuses on skills first, adding content second. This approach squanders the early childhood learning window, which is evident

---

[39] She will readily admit this. It turns out I am married to one of the Bene Gesserit.

[40] The chapter QR includes the *Wikipedia* article on the word gap.

in the low reading proficiency of lower-income students by 3rd grade.

The differences are stark. In the San Francisco Unified School District, only 20% of Black 3rd graders meet or exceed reading standards. By 8th grade, only 22% do.[41] These students are effectively lost by 3rd grade. Once lost, they require hundreds of hours of one-on-one instruction or its equivalent to catch up, as Jeb's story illustrates.

So, how do we actually improve the reading curriculum and ability of our schools? I propose two ideas.

Idea 1: Identify a handful of schools with key early-grades teachers and leadership who are enthusiastic about participating in a pilot program in partnership with the California Department of Education. Curriculum developers from the CDE could begin with a content-rich baseline curriculum (e.g., those of the Core Knowledge Foundation), and adapt it for the pilot schools.[42] They would provide detailed student materials, training resources, lesson plans, and instructional support.

Pilot schools could phase in the program with a Kindergarten cohort, following them through 3rd grade and the first set of standardized test scores. This would allow for empirical measurement of outcomes under this approach. With routine efficacy measurement and quality improvement processes, the CDE could develop a high-quality model curriculum and make it widely accessible to other schools.

Given the extensive social science research on this topic, there is every reason to expect a measurable difference. If such results were achieved, they could be highlighted to encourage organic adoption of the approach in other schools. As more positive outcomes accumulate, public pressure could accelerate the spread of the program, in effect using the politics of the situation to drive change rather than stymie it. Additionally, the CDE could offer the curriculum and resources to districts at low cost, providing

---

[41] This data is sourced from the California Assessment of Student Performance and Progress website and is available in the chapter QR.

[42] The chapter QR includes a link to the Core Knowledge Foundation. They have done great work developing a content-rich curriculum targeting those young ages when kids can absorb content quickly.

an alternative to expensive corporate curriculum developers, in effect using money to help drive change, rather than stymie it.

Idea 2: Identify another group of schools, ideally with high concentrations of low-income kids, to run a different pilot project. In California, minors as young as 14 can legally work, so in this pilot, the schools would identify all the 14–18-year-old students who are strong readers, in the opinion of the English teachers at the schools. These students would be offered the opportunity to stay after school and read to small groups of younger kids and be paid for it. There are some schools out there that have *kids read to kids* initiatives, but I am not aware of any that pay the kids who do the reading.

The fact is, the student readers would be doing something socially valuable, and giving of their time to do it, so they should be paid for it. Moreover, when programs like this are offered only on a volunteer basis, we naturally exclude kids whose families are not wealthy enough to allow them the luxury of resumé-padding volunteer time. The CDE has plenty of discretionary funds that an effective and innovative Superintendent could use to create a grant program for interested districts to use in paying their student-readers. The program would reward students for being good enough at reading to be selected to be a reader and would give them paid work experience, which is good for them and for society.

Meanwhile, the younger kids, who are almost certainly not being read to as much as their higher-income peers, would have the chance to close some of that gap. Their attendance would be rigorously tracked, so that their future test results could be evaluated against the amount of time they had spent in the after-school reading program, allowing us to evaluate the effectiveness of the program. If the program were shown to be effective, the grant program could be expanded to more schools over time.

Both of these ideas are largely within the executive purview of the Superintendent and the CDE, thereby bypassing the endless wait for legislative action. Of course, the Superintendent of Public Instruction has, in recent history, been inhabited by politicians who serve largely as tools of the legislature and the state Board of Education. But, a more engaged and energetic leadership could, without doubt, implement proposals to dramatically improve the literacy of our children in public schools.

How *You* Can Help

There are lots of ways you can be a positive force for reading in kids' lives.

Basic level:

Start with getting to know the performance of your own school district in teaching reading. Once you have a handle on that, compare your district to some nearby districts. The chapter QR includes the site where you can easily look up this data. I have also placed a short video there showing you how to use it.

Next, listen to the podcast *Sold a Story*. It is included in the chapter QR. If you are solo, it's a good thing for your commute or for a walk or workout. If you are part of a group, listen to one episode per group meeting. Pause it periodically and have a group discussion:

- What surprised you?
- What did not surprise you?
- How did you feel when you learned how decisions about teaching reading were made?

Advocate for evidence-based literacy instruction at your local or countywide school board meetings. Give a public comment in support of this and use the statistics you gathered above to help bolster your case. Remember: polite-but-firm is the sweet spot!

Intermediate level:

Volunteer with a local nonprofit organization that focuses on education; many of them have opportunities to work with kids on reading. For example, in my area we are fortunate to have the Cabrillo Education Foundation (CEF), which does great work and has many different volunteer opportunities. The chapter QR includes a link to CEF. If you have a good organization in your area, send their website to me at gus@AisforAvg.com and I will compile them by county. Make it easier for the next person to find a volunteer opportunity!

Organize a book drive or a fundraiser to raise money for a school to purchase decodable books or professional development for its teachers. Remember, many teachers were never taught about the science of reading, and raising money to get them professional development can be a great way to accelerate the process of transitioning to more evidence-based reading approaches. Contact schools in your area to see who needs this kind of help. Remember that the high-needs schools are your point of biggest impact.

Jedi level:

Network with a community-based organization in your area; faith communities are an obvious choice, but rotary clubs, lion's clubs, elks lodges, and so forth are also good options. From there, reach out to a community-based organization in a high-needs area and start to build a relationship between your organization and theirs. Once you have a warm connection between the two organizations, organize a weekly trip that takes early reading-age kids from the high needs organization to a local retirement home, and pair up each of the kids with 1 or 2 retirees to have the kids read to them. Most folks in retirement homes do not have many visitors, so they will be glad for the company, and the kids get a captive audience to practice their reading skills on. Everyone wins!

Getting something like this going takes a lot of networking and willingness to talk to people, plus the capacity to endure some false starts. Moreover, you will want to get a big enough group of adults involved in this that the logistics do not fall too heavily on any one person. That is a lot of organizational work, and very few people have the skills and the fortitude to do it. It takes a special kind of person to make it happen. Be that person! That's Jedi level.

* * *

Chapter 8 QR code

Once you learn to read, you will be forever free.
– Frederick Douglass

9

Math is Hard! (for California)

Without mathematics, there's nothing you can do. Everything around you is mathematics. Everything around you is numbers.
– Shakuntala Devi

* * *

I have been teaching math for 22 years, but my teaching career really started back in 7th grade. I was part of a multiyear, outside-of-school program for gifted math students called Mathematics Education for Gifted Secondary School Students (MEGSSS).[43] To get in, I had to take the SAT math section as a 5th grader. It was a wonderful program; its approach to teaching math resembles what happens in regular school to about the same degree that Mandarin resembles English (i.e., not at all). But the downside of being in it was that math class at school quickly became boring, and I have never handled boredom well, then or now.

Consequently, I was something of a problem for my 7th grade math teacher, Ms. Herlihy. And she had two other problems as well: Charles and Orin,

---

[43] The chapter QR includes a link to the MEGSSS website. It is a phenomenal program for any mathematically precocious child. The curriculum is designed to conceptually introduce abstract and advanced topics to young kids.

legendary class clowns capable of derailing a class in a truly dizzying array of ways. One day, in a fit of pique at something Orin had done, Ms. Herlihy looked me dead in the eye and said, "You. Take Charles and Orin to that table in the back and teach them this," pointing at whatever was on the chalkboard.

At the time, I thought Ms. Herlihy was crazy. But the three of us accepted our banishment to the back of the room, and for lack of anything better to do, I spent the rest of the year privately tutoring Charles and Orin. Though I originally thought her idea was insane, years later, I realized Ms. Herlihy was actually a genius. In one move, she got rid of all three of her biggest problems. Charles and Orin learned far more math, I found something fulfilling to do during class, and Ms. Herlihy was able to focus on teaching everyone else.

That was my gateway to teaching in general and teaching math in particular. I have taught math to over 1,000 kids over the years, and in all that time the question students have asked the most is "Why do I even need to learn this?" Given that our discussion on the improvement of public schools began with the question, "Should we even have public schools?" it seems fitting that the first question answered in a discussion about the improvement of math education should be, "Should we even teach math?"

While I am not aware of any mainstream movement advocating against the teaching of math *entirely*, there are plenty of folks who advocate for teaching only those math skills required for basic daily life. Andrew Hacker, author of *The Math Myth*,[44] argues that we should abandon traditional math classes like Algebra or Calculus and focus instead on numeracy.[45] Numeracy can be understood as the mathematical equivalent of literacy—the ability to conceptualize and apply simple numerical concepts. Here again we see that *A is for Average* mentality: the suggestion is to dumb everything down to a few simple concepts and then pat ourselves on the back for the bold progress we've made.

Of course, it is trivially true that all students should develop numeracy

---

[44] The *Wikipedia* article on *The Math Myth* is available in the chapter QR. This article highlights well the shortsightedness of Hacker's argument.

[45] The chapter QR includes a link to the *Wikipedia* article on numeracy.

skills. I am also a serious supporter of teaching kids related concepts such as financial literacy.[46] However, not giving kids any exposure to advanced math is misguided at best. The vast majority of students will never need to understand the significance of class uprisings in medieval Europe, differentiate between kingdom, order, and phylum, or analyze archetypes in an Elizabethan-era play. Yet, we still expose children to world history, biology, and Shakespeare. We teach these subjects, not because they are strictly necessary for daily adult life, but because they develop the core skills needed to achieve success: critical thinking, communication, logic, and the ability to learn new things.

The teaching of math advances the same goals.

When students protest *why do I need to know this?* I counter with a question of my own: "What is the one thing that the job market rewards over all else?" Students have various answers to this question, but I continue asking probing questions until we arrive at the real answer: the ability to problem-solve. In general, the pay one receives in the job market is correlated with the complexity of the problems one is solving.

When you leave your trash on the curb, the person who picks it up and takes it to the landfill likely receives low compensation relative to other professions. The problem they solve is not particularly complex; the level of skill and training required to perform the job is low relative to a lot of other professions. To be clear, the work is physically demanding and absolutely critical to public health, which makes it an *important* problem to solve (notice how bad it gets when sanitation workers go on strike), but relatively speaking it is not a *complex* problem to solve.

Contrast that, say, with conducting a successful neurosurgical operation. Neurosurgeons are well-paid in their attending life because the task of opening up a person's skull up and doing something useful in there without killing them is an especially complex problem to solve. Because of the

---

[46] I taught financial literacy to low-income, inner-city youth in Richmond, VA, through program known as Junior Achievement. If you are looking for a volunteer organization, I highly recommend them. The chapter QR includes a link to the Junior Achievement site; I encourage you to connect with your local chapter.

complexity of the problem, not many people can solve it, and so not many people can become neurosurgeons. Because of that scarcity, neurosurgeons have a great deal of bargaining power in the job market, and they make good money.

Similarly, running a company profitably is a hard problem to solve. Determining reliably which startup companies will be successful is a hard problem to solve. Thus, not many people are qualified to do these things, and those who can are paid handsomely. This is even more true in entertainment: reliably hitting a 95 mile-per-hour fastball, skillfully singing the *Queen of the Night* aria, or being a bankable Hollywood actor are all complex problems to solve. Regardless of how important one considers solving entertainment problems to be, people enjoy seeing them solved, and not many people can solve them well. Thus, not many people can be professional baseball players, opera singers, or movie stars, and the resulting scarcity leads to good compensation.

That is why it is so important to learn math. Math will not help you hit a fastball, sing an aria, or be a Hollywood star, but there are only a handful of jobs for those things anyway. There are millions of jobs, though, in business, law, medicine, government, STEM, and so on, and being a better problem solver will help you excel in any of those fields. Math, it turns out, is just distilled problem-solving, and becoming better at it makes you better at problem-solving in general.

Research from the Federal Reserve Bank of Cleveland examined how studying math affects students' outcomes in the labor market, especially for those who do not go on to college.[47] The findings were striking: for both high school dropouts and graduates, stronger math preparation led to better employment rates and higher earnings. In fact, for high school graduates, the earnings difference between students with strong versus weak math backgrounds was roughly equivalent to the financial return of completing an additional year of college. In other words, students who never set foot on a college campus could still earn substantially more money simply by taking more math in high school, a place where the tuition cost is zero (at a public

---

[47] The study is included in the chapter QR.

high school, of course).

A second study, conducted by the National Bureau of Economic Research, looked at how increasing math course requirements affected long-term earnings.[48] The researchers found that when states raised those requirements, Black high school graduates saw their adult earnings increase by 3–4%. The additional math did not make students more likely to attend college, but it did move them into jobs that demanded higher cognitive skills, and those jobs paid more. Notably, this relationship did not appear for other subjects; the effect was specific to math.

I highlight the results for Black students deliberately. Many of the *A is for Average* policies, including weakening or eliminating math requirements, are promoted in the name of "equity." Yet the evidence shows the opposite: strengthening math education actually narrows the earnings gap. If equity truly matters, then one should advocate for *more* math, not less.

But, *which* math?

For those of you who are not deep in the weeds of education policy, it may surprise you to learn that the question of *which* math is taught to kids is quite controversial and starkly *political.* I went through school in the seventies and eighties, when the focus of math was on its procedural elements. This approach emphasized memorizing math facts and learning procedures to solve various categories of problems. A deep understanding of the concepts underlying the procedures and categories of problems was less explicitly emphasized.

This approach did have some strengths. For instance, it is useful to know multiplication tables. These days, when I ask a student "what is nine times six?" they will often respond with a series of mental gymnastics: "Well, nine is ten minus one. So, nine times six is really ten minus one, all times six. And that's ten times six minus one times six. And that's sixty minus six, and sixty minus six is fifty four. So, nine times six is fifty four!" Strictly speaking, that

---

[48] The study is included in the chapter QR.

is true, and the ability to conceptualize nine as ten minus one has some real utility in more complex calculations. That said, it is also useful to just *know* that nine times six is fifty four.

The procedural approach to math is also useful in that most real-world problem solving, the kind you would do at a regular, real-world job, involves the application of rules and procedures to categories of problems. Thus, training your mind to think procedurally in this manner is practically useful, even if the specific problems you learn to solve in math class are not the exact problems you would be working on in the real world.

Of course, the procedural approach does have weaknesses. Its principal weakness is that, if a math teacher is not careful, it calcifies into a sort of "stimulus-response math." In stimulus-response math, kids learn procedures, but they never learn *why* they are doing those procedural steps. Instead, they learn to recognize the correct response to a particular stimulus (e.g. the structure of a word problem). This is problematic, for example, in a standardized testing environment that is designed to pressure-test a student's conceptual understanding of a topic: if the concept is tested using a question type the student has not previously seen, then a student who has only learned stimulus-response math is lost at sea; because they have never seen that exact stimulus before, they have no idea what the proper response is.

I receive calls like this from parents all the time: "I don't get it! My kid has gotten nothing but straight As in math, so I just don't understand why his SAT math score is so low." Well, why might that be?

First, remember that, at this point, *A is for Average*; i.e., getting an A in a math class does not necessarily indicate any special mastery of content. Second, there a good chance the student is approaching math in a stimulus-response kind of way, and it is not hard for the test developers over at the College Board to come up with a question structure that student has never seen before. Then, presented with a completely new stimulus, the student has no idea what the correct response should be.

In the early nineties, math education underwent a major philosophical shift. The old procedural approach of memorizing math facts and practicing algorithms was increasingly criticized as too narrow. In 1989, the National Council of Teachers of Mathematics released its *Curriculum and Evaluation Standards for School Mathematics*, which became the foundation for what educators called "reform math." This approach emphasized conceptual understanding, reasoning, and multiple solution strategies over rote memorization and procedural fluency.

Textbooks and curricula influenced by the reform math standards, such as *Everyday Mathematics* and *Investigations in Number, Data, and Space*, began appearing in schools across the country, including California. Memorizing multiplication tables and practicing standard algorithms was de-emphasized, and the goal became helping students develop a deeper conceptual grasp of mathematics.

However, by the mid-to-late nineties, this shift sparked a strong backlash, which came to be known as the math wars. Parents, mathematicians, and even some educators argued that students were losing essential skills and that procedural fluency was being abandoned in favor of abstract reasoning. California, in particular, became a hotbed for these debates. The state's *Math Frameworks of 1992* reflected a strong conceptual focus, while the 1997 framework swung back sharply in the other direction.

More recent movements in the 2000s and 2010s like Common Core mathematics have attempted to (somewhat) nationally standardize curriculum, but have failed to resolve the fundamental debates over what math is best for teaching to kids. A thoughtful approach to teaching mathematics would balance *both* procedural accuracy with conceptual understanding, but right now, schools across the state (and even the nation), have decided that even memorizing basic multiple tables is "boring" and, therefore, not worthy of doing.

As our school system becomes increasingly hostile to any kind of procedural assessment, students find themselves in a position where as long as they demonstrate a conceptual grasp of the content, little or no consequence is applied for making procedural errors. That is part of why they suffer on standardized math tests: they make easily predictable procedural errors, which have no consequence at school, but which lead to the incorrect answer choices on the test.

When I train students and they get a question wrong for this reason, they will often say something along the lines of "Oh, well, I understood the problem. I get it!" I then have to remind them how standardized testing works in the real world: "I see that you get it, but you didn't get it *right*." Some students accept this correction in stride, but others have truly bought into the idea that accuracy is not as important as understanding, and they protest.

With these students, I try to paint a picture for them. I received my MBA from the Yale School of Management, and some years ahead of me was Indra Nooyi, CEO of PepsiCo from 2006 until 2018. I ask my students to imagine that I secured for them an internship with Indra and that she sent them an email instructing them to create a presentation with recommendations for how to increase PepsiCo's share of the Austrian soda market.

Then, I ask my students: "If you show up on Monday and deliver a detailed, compelling presentation of how to increase PepsiCo's share of the *Australian* soda market, what do you think is more likely to happen? Is she going to pat you on the head and say, 'What's important here is that you *conceptually understand* how to increase market share? Or is she going to fire you on the spot for your inability to follow simple instructions?"

I pose this hypothetical to underscore for students that in the real world outcomes do, in fact, matter, however much schools may pretend they don't. Of course, the corollary to that *A is for Average* mindset, that philosophy that outcomes don't matter, is *therefore, get rid of tests and assessments that measure outcomes.* Math is the canary in the coal mine with respect to that movement.

So, when we think about how to improve our school system, which (rightly) leaves decisions like *what kind of math should our kids learn?* largely to the local level, statewide leadership is still needed. The California Department of Education is well within its authority to develop and champion a curriculum that balances the conceptual and procedural aspects of math, and that insists on a solid grounding of math facts and procedural fluency coupled with conceptual understanding and measured through rigorous assessments.

An example of a curriculum inspired by a successful national model is

Singapore Math, the program my team and I typically use when working with younger students.[49] It is based on the math framework developed by Singapore's Ministry of Education, which has consistently produced world-class results. The curriculum strikes an excellent balance between conceptual and procedural learning. For evidence that this approach works, take a look at the PISA (Programme for International Student Assessment)[50] results by country, where students from Singapore routinely rank at or near the top of the world.[51]

Rank	Country	Score
1	Singapore	575
2	Macau	552
3	Taiwan	547
4	Hong Kong	540
5	Japan	536
...		
33	Malta	466
34	United States	465
35	Slovakia	464

We barely edge out Slovakia, one of the poorest countries in Europe.

If we want to improve outcomes here in California and prepare our kids to compete in a global job market, then we need leadership that will push back on the trend toward well-intentioned, but fundamentally misguided, math

---

[49] The chapter QR includes a link to the Singapore Math site, which I strongly recommend. I would also clarify that neither I personally nor Advantage Testing broadly has any financial relationship with Singapore Math; I recommend it solely on its merits.

[50] The chapter QR includes the PISA website if you would like to learn more.

[51] The chapter QR includes both a link to these results.

curricula. It has been quite a while since we had that kind of leadership in the California Department of Education.

In sum

California's performance as a state in teaching math is embarrassing relative to the rest of America, and America's performance as a country is embarrassing relative to the rest of the world. But that fate is not written in stone. We *can* improve, by pushing for more math and for more advanced math for all students and persuading schools to employ math curricula that are clearly successful.

Otherwise, our lower-income student population will continue to be left behind, while the higher-income student population will just continue to get what they need outside the school system (for instance, by coming to me and my team). But there is no reason why it must be that way! We can make better choices as a state, and we can choose better leaders to make those choices.

How *You* Can Help

There are plenty of ways you can get involved in the issue of improving our state's performance in math.

Basic level:

Help get kids excited in STEM topics. Consider using your social media presence: follow social media accounts that promote interest and excitement around math. The chapter QR will take you to my website, where I have posted a few that I have found. If you find some you think are good, send them to me at gus@AisforAvg.com (or use the contact form on my website).

Attend STEM events at your local schools. As with social media, your attendance can help build a sense of energy and excitement around math. The kids and teachers will appreciate you, and you might also learn some cool things!

Intermediate level:

Monitor your local board meeting agendas and look for opportunities to give public comments in support of rigorous math curricula. When you see something coming up on the agenda, organize some other folks to also show up and give public comments. The more people, the better! It creates the pressure that is more likely to produce the outcomes you want.

If you have a job that requires a lot of quantitative work, volunteer to be a class speaker for a math class at a local school. You can talk about your own experience and the role math plays in your work. If students hear from more people that math is critical to success in the job market, they will be more motivated to apply themselves to the study of math.

Write a letter to the editor in support of more rigorous math curricula. Point to something about your local school, either something they're doing well with math education or something they are doing poorly, and use that as the crux of your letter.

Note: If you going to use AI in your writing, I recommend you write your draft first and have AI clean it up, rather than have AI write it from scratch. AI's writing is so bland, it may well make it less likely that an editor chooses your submission. Your local newspaper's website will have guidelines published for how to submit, maximum word counts, etc. Be sure to follow them.

Jedi level:

My organization's foundation has a partnership with MIT and with Jane Street Capital that sponsors the world's largest math competition for girls. If you want to experience some incredibly difficult math questions, the chapter QR will take you to the website for the Advantage Testing Foundation/Jane Street Math Prize for Girls. There, if you click "Resources" and then "Previous Exams," you will find some math problems that will curl your socks. It is fun being part of an organization that helps foster math in this way.

Here is your Jedi task: organize a math contest for your local school. Choose whatever grade makes sense for you (though in general I would recommend middle or high school, since the kids younger than that have not learned much math yet.) Your contest doesn't need to have the world's largest prize, and the prize or prizes don't even have to be monetary; if you and all your friends pitch in, you will definitely be able to put together something to get the kids excited!

Split the work up: someone coordinates with the school, someone sources the questions and answers, someone organizes sourcing the prize(s), and someone puts together the team that will grade the kids' work and tally up the results on contest day. But, at the root of all this is someone who is willing to assemble that team of people. That is the Jedi master. Be that person!

* * *

Chapter 9 QR code

Mathematics knows no races or geographic boundaries;
for mathematics, the cultural world is one country.
– David Hilbert

10

History and Ethnic Studies

History is the version of past events that people have decided to agree upon.
- Napoleon Bonaparte

* * *

St. Louis, 1982

When I was ten, the doorbell rang. I opened the door, and there was an older man standing there. He looked at me and asked, "Is your mother home?" So I did what any kid in the eighties would do and I yelled through the house (we had no messaging apps back then), "Hey Mom, some guy is here to see you!"

My mom came rushing to the door, and the moment she saw him, she exclaimed, "Dad?" and ran into his arms. It turned out this was my grandfather, a grandfather I did not even know existed.

Grandpa had spent years working on oil fields in Saudi Arabia and Libya. In 1982, President Reagan ordered all Americans out of Libya because of escalating tensions and banned Libyan oil imports. So, Grandpa left the Middle East and came home to the United States. He had made enough money overseas to travel widely, and he was a gifted storyteller. He had a treasure trove of stories about the world he had seen, and I hung on his every word.

Kids have a funny way of questioning tiny things (*Why is the inside of a pineapple yellow?*) while unquestioningly accepting large-scale aspects of their realities. For example, until the day my grandpa turned up on our doorstep, I'd never really thought about the fact that every other kid had a grandma and a grandpa, but I had a grandma and an uncle (my grandma lived on my uncle's farm).

You may be wondering why grandpa's existence had never come up before. Here's his story: Grandpa grew up on a farm in southern Illinois. Like most of his brothers, he went off to fight in World War II. Grandpa's other two brothers who went to war joined the Army; one even drove a tank under General Patton. But grandpa joined the Air Force instead.

The military gave him an escape from the farm, and it triggered a real wanderlust in him. When the war ended, he tried to settle down with my grandma (she had been a waitress in a restaurant he'd frequented, and I guess she couldn't resist a dashing young man in uniform), but the wanderlust was firmly in him by then and he discovered that he chafed at the idea of spending the rest of his life on the farm, as his parents and grandparents had. That frustration manifested itself in a lot of unhealthy ways: heavy drinking (he was a functioning alcoholic for at least 60 years) and running around on my grandma. Finally, one day when my mom was 7 years old, he came home and announced he was leaving, and he looked at my mom and said, "You can come with me, or you can stay with her." Mom, being *seven*, decided to stay with my grandma, and so grandpa walked out the door and didn't come back until he turned up on our doorstep 30 years later, in 1982.

The reason I told you this story is that it has to do with the question of how we should teach history, a question that is extremely divisive in today's world. In thinking about my grandpa, there are three ways you could think of him:

1. He was a well-traveled, gifted storyteller, with immense intellectual curiosity about every subject you can imagine, a person who wouldn't hesitate to buy you a meal and regale you with amazing stories, and a person who devotedly took care of my grandma in her final days the way you think every husband should (they never actually divorced, because doing so was really complicated in the fifties).

2. He was a philandering alcoholic who walked out on his wife and daughter and didn't look back for 30 years.
3. He was a complicated human being, simultaneously capable of immense generosity of spirit and immense selfishness.

What I have done is to present you with the facts of his story, and I'm leaving it to you to decide which of those three interpretations you choose. If something in your worldview makes you say, "He really came around in the end, and redemption is important, so I'm willing to overlook the bad stuff," then that's fine! That's a reasonable interpretation. If something in your background makes you say, "I just cannot get past the fact that he walked out on his family; he's dead to me," that's also reasonable! If you're curious where I come down on this question, it's option #3, that he was complicated, as I suspect all of us are if you dig deep enough. I choose to appreciate and cherish what was great about him, while also never forgetting what was very much not great about him.

This story speaks to the heart of how we should teach subjects like history and ethnic studies, a question that is currently the subject of some titanic battles in the public sphere. For instance, there are many academics who make a convincing case that very little evidence exists to support the claims that proponents of ethnic studies often make about the supposed benefits to students of taking an ethnic studies class. In a January 2021 letter to current Superintendent of Public Instruction Tony Thurmond, over two dozen academics began by stating:

> *We are university scholars and academics, many of us with decades of experience designing and carrying out empirical research and qualified to analyze scholarly publications. We are deeply concerned with the misrepresentation of social science research that is used to support claims of the benefits of ethnic studies courses in the Introduction and Overview to the Third Field Review of the Ethnic Studies Model*

Curriculum (ESMC).[52]

But since teaching ethnic studies is now a statutory requirement in California, we should discuss how best to teach it. I think the answer to that question is actually simple. Let's illustrate the answer using the example of George Washington.

A good history class, which of course will not have time to present a deep dive into the life of George Washington, would present a subset of facts that give a sense of the complexity of the man.[53] For instance, here are a couple:

1. As our first President, he voluntarily walked away from power after two terms in office, when most everyone around him wanted him to go for a third term, and thereby set an important precedent for the peaceful, voluntary transfer of power between Presidents.
2. The willingness to voluntarily walk away from that level of power is extraordinarily rare in political history.
3. He owned other human beings, in flagrant violation of the principles he so nobly fought for and upon which our country was founded.
4. His failure to lead on the issue of slavery, though thoroughly unremarkable for his time in history and his station in society, is nevertheless thrown into stark relief by some of his contemporaries, e.g. John Adams,[54] who found their way to the correct position on the issue.

---

[52] The chapter QR has a link to the full letter. The authors deconstruct claims made in the model curriculum about its supposed benefits, and they do so in a very detailed way. I highly recommend reading the letter.

[53] For an excellent biography on George Washington, one that does the deep dive but is also very readable and engaging, I highly recommend *His Excellency George Washington*, by Joseph Ellis. The chapter QR will take you to a link to it.

[54] John and Abigail Adams are my favorite presidential couple. Enough of their letters to each other have survived that we have an excellent window into the richness of their relationship. For a phenomenal biography of John Adams, I recommend *John Adams*, by David McCullough (the chapter QR will take you to a link to it.) Actually, if you enjoy reading about history, you should just read everything David McCullough has ever written. You won't regret doing that.

A student would walk out of a good history class with a command of a representative set of facts like this and with the ability to use these facts to articulate persuasively the case for why a reasonable, thoughtful person would, in fact, want to honor George Washington and name things after him, and the case for why a reasonable, thoughtful person would not, in fact, want to honor George Washington and name things after him. An educated person can articulate clearly both points of view.

The one thing a good history class absolutely would NOT do is say that one or the other of those perspectives is the "correct" perspective. The moment a school crosses that line is the moment the school has not only unambiguously exceeded its authority but also abused the public's trust in establishing compulsory education.

Thus, while there is a clear theoretical case for having history and ethnic studies be part of the curriculum that all kids get exposed to, it is critical that these subjects be taught in a manner that is consistent with the public's trust that the school system will not abuse its authority; i.e., it's critical that these subjects be taught in a values-neutral way. The CDE could and should lead on this issue by developing a model curriculum that gives clear guidance on how to teach these subjects values-neutrally.

Unfortunately, the CDE has abdicated its responsibility to lead by example by instead creating a model curriculum that is anything but values-neutral. Let's engage critically with the existing model curriculum, which runs to 696 pages and takes quite some time to read.[55] We'll start on page 10:

> *Furthermore, considering that European American-centered history and cultures are already robustly taught in the school curriculum, ethnic studies presents an opportunity for more inclusive and diverse histories and cultures to be highlighted and studied in a manner that is meaningful and can be transformative for all students.*

---

[55] Reading the model curriculum was even more tedious than it sounds. But no need to take my word for it; the chapter QR will take you to a link to the model curriculum if you'd like to decide for yourself.

It's worth noting that "European American-centered history" is not the only thing "robustly taught" within the existing school curriculum. Here are just a few examples from the October, 1998, History–Social Science Content Standards:[56]

- **HSS-1.5.2 (Grade 1):** Understand the ways in which American Indians and immigrants have helped define California and American culture.
- **HSS-2.5 (Grade 2):** Students understand the importance of individual action and character and explain how heroes from long ago and the recent past have made a difference in others' lives (e.g., from biographies of Abraham Lincoln, Louis Pasteur, Sitting Bull, George Washington Carver, Marie Curie, Albert Einstein, Golda Meir, Jackie Robinson, Sally Ride).
- **HSS-3.4.6 (Grade 3):** Describe the lives of American heroes who took risks to secure our freedoms (e.g., Anne Hutchinson, Benjamin Franklin, Thomas Jefferson, Abraham Lincoln, Frederick Douglass, Harriet Tubman, Martin Luther King, Jr.).
- **HSS-4.2.1 (Grade 4):** Discuss the major nations of the California Indians, including their geographic distribution, economic activities, legends, and religious beliefs; and describe how they depended on, adapted to, and modified the physical environment by cultivation of land and use of sea resources.
- **HSS-5.4.6 (Grade 5):** Describe the introduction of slavery into America, the responses of slave families to their condition, the ongoing struggle between proponents and opponents of slavery, and the gradual institutionalization of slavery in the South.
- **HSS-6.4 (Grade 6):** Students analyze the geographic, political, economic, religious, and social structures of the early civilizations of India.
- **HSS-7.2 (Grade 7):** Students analyze the geographic, political, economic, religious, and social structures of the civilizations of Islam in the Middle Ages.
- **HSS-8.11.2 (Grade 8):** Identify the push-pull factors in the movement of

[56] The chapter QR will take you to a link to the CDE's history and social studies standards.

former slaves to the cities in the North and to the West and their differing experiences in those regions (e.g., the experiences of Buffalo Soldiers).

As you can see from just this sample, there is quite a bit of nonwhite, non-European perspective in the core history and social studies. The rhetoric of the model ethnic studies curriculum suggests that it is perfectly suited to address how history and social studies were taught in the sixties. But it's not especially well-suited to address how history and social studies are taught *today.*

Nevertheless, there's nothing intrinsically wrong with a class that focuses on non-white, non-European history. The problem comes when only one side is presented on an issue where reasonable people could be on either side. The model curriculum mentions the importance of "counternarratives," but a counternarrative is not a counternarrative if it is the *only* narrative presented. For example, at multiple points in the model curriculum, the phrase "exploitative economic systems" is used, and it is used as a proxy for "capitalism." We know that this is the case because an advisor to the development of the model curriculum wrote a public letter in which she lamented that the word "capitalism" had been changed to "exploitative economic systems."[57]

It is an abuse of the public trust to present capitalism as intrinsically "exploitative"; an educated person should be able to argue either side of a debate about whether capitalism is intrinsically good or bad. The only way to accomplish this is to present both sides of the debate and have the students practice arguing each. Yes, students should know about wealth inequality today and the destabilizing effect that extreme levels of wealth inequality have had on societies throughout history. But they should also know that the ability to pool capital has led to most of the technological developments that have made it possible for human life to grow and thrive:

[57] The chapter QR will take you to a link to the letter if you would like to read it.

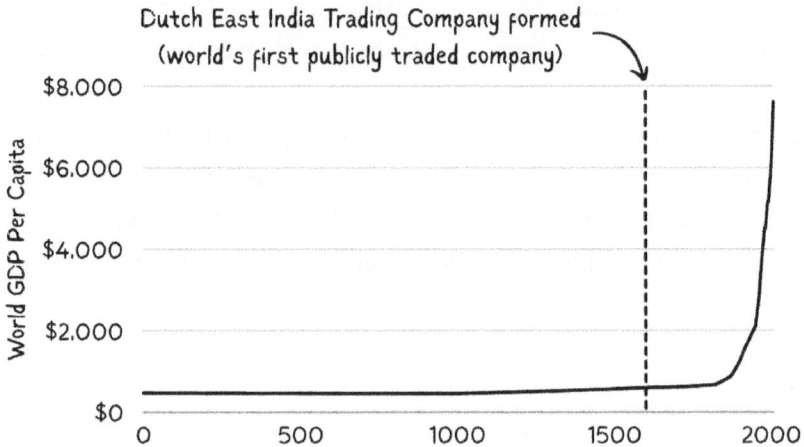

Yes, students should know about the constant tension between labor and capital, the way power has ebbed and flowed between them at different times and in different societies, and the strategies each has used in its struggle with the other. But they should also know that China's and India's embrace of capitalism has allowed them to lift hundreds of millions of people out of extreme poverty in only a generation, an unprecedented accomplishment in human history.

A well-executed, values-neutral ethnic studies class would present capitalism in its full complexity, and then *let the students decide for themselves* whether capitalism is intrinsically good, intrinsically bad, or somewhere in between.[58] The class would *not* put its thumb on the scale in either direction.

We can see this same dynamic at play in the model curriculum's approach to social justice. On page 459 the model curriculum states, "The focus of unit 4 will be to provide students with models of social justice movements to guide their own social justice initiatives." The models listed include:

- Women
- African Americans
- LGBTQ+

---

[58] This is the most accurate assessment, in my opinion. But of course, you must judge for yourself.

- The Brown Berets
- Asian-American Nationalism
- The American Indian Movement

And later, on page 558:

- The immigrant rights movement
- Black Lives Matter movement
- Environmental justice movements
- Feminist movements
- LGBTQIA movements

These are all indeed social justice movements. What they have in common is that they are all social justice movements that are approved by the same one slice of the American political spectrum. There is no mention, for instance, of the temperance movement, which was driven by political conservatives and which had a significant impact on US politics. Or consider the issue of the US-Mexican border. On page 647, a suggested class exercise begins with the prompt, "The border is…" and then some sample statements are given. Here are the first three (the others are all similar to these):

- "For Mexico, the border is not that rigid Puritan thing, a line; straight lines are unknown in Mexico. The border, like everything else, is subject to supply and demand. The border is a revolving door." - Richard Rodriguez
- "The border is transient . . . the border is a word game . . . the border is a virtual cesspool" - *The Atlantic Monthly*
- "Many Mexicans think of the move from Cd. Juárez across the Rio Grande more like moving to a richer neighborhood than going to another country." - *The Washington Post*, 1978

The sample statements provided all represent one basic view of the border. But there is another view of the border, one that approximately half the Latino community voted for in the most recent presidential election. Here are three representative quotes from Latinos expressing that contrasting perspective:[59]

- "As a Latino AmericanI want American citizens to be put first; all immigration should be halted until this government takes seriously the threat of illegal immigration." –Chris Salcedo, conservative talk radio host, Texas
- "How you could justify disrespecting our immigration laws, violating our national sovereignty without permission of our nation... That to me sounds illegitimate." –Reymundo Torres, President, Arizona Latino Republican Association
- "They do want immigration reform... But they also do not believe that you should be able to come to the border as easily as has happened in the past." –Rubén Gallego, Democratic Senator, on sentiment in the working-class Latino community

It took approximately three minutes of my time to produce this contrasting perspective on an issue of great political salience in our country. Thus, we can be sure that the choice to present only one side of this issue was deliberate, and it was *political*. And it's emblematic of a process that has produced a 696-page document which is impressive primarily in the extent to which it is ideologically monochromatic. The irony in that is particularly sharp given how many times the model curriculum laments, as it says on page 98, "the silencing of alternative accounts," and how often it speaks of challenging dominant narratives by, as it says on page 352, "presenting experiences and perspectives from diverse voices."

The price of producing such a politically motivated document, one that silences the perspectives of approximately half the population, is the steady erosion of support for public education. This is as unfortunate as it is unnecessary. California's students deserve a model ethnic studies curriculum

---

[59] The chapter QR will take you to links to the articles giving these quotes.

that honors the public's trust by remaining as values-neutral as possible, but achieving that goal would require revising the existing model curriculum, which in turn would require new, better leadership at the California Department of Education. Until then, the best we can do is stay vigilant and engaged in the decisions our local school boards make about history and ethnic studies and what curriculum they will use.

How *You* Can Help

There are lots of ways you can get involved in the issue of improving how our kids learn history and ethnic studies:

Basic level:

Attend any school board meeting where curriculum around history, social studies, or ethnic studies are on the agenda and be prepared to give a polite-but-firm public comment in support of a values-neutral curriculum.

Do you have a child going through a history, social studies, or ethnic studies class? Check in with your child each day to see what they learned about. If anything seems particularly reasonable or praiseworthy, put it on social media. If anything seems over the line, carefully and as descriptively as possible put *that* on social media. Instead of telling people what the answer is, ask a question like, "Do you agree that this is appropriate for my kid's class?"

Intermediate level:

Volunteer with a local school; there are many different forms this could take. You could help with any history-related events or fairs. You could be a guest speaker at a history class and share your perspective on your own experience or the experience of your family and how these experiences inform your views on what it means to be American or to be a member of your community. You could help organize a panel discussion for a history or ethnic studies class, and you can be a force that helps ensure a broad range of perspectives is represented on the panel.

If you have children going through the school system, take careful note of what the history/social studies/ethnic studies classes are teaching your kids. If a class strays over the line of what's reasonable, take some detailed notes on why. When you've got two examples, you have enough for a good op-ed: for each of your two cases, carefully lay out the facts of what happened, then offer an affirmative vision of how the class could have accomplished what it set out to do in a better way. It's important to provide that affirmative vision so that your piece doesn't just sound like it's complaining. You'll have a better chance of getting your op-ed published.

If you don't have kids, find a likeminded person who does and partner up with them. Keeping track of this stuff is actually real work, and so your partner in this effort will appreciate the help. If neither one of you feels confident as a writer, rope in a third person who has that skill. A small team is going to be both more fun and better able to manage the workload of monitoring what's going on. But it's important work! Most of what happens in a classroom is fine, but the small fraction of stuff that isn't manages to slip by under the radar most of the time. You can be a force to make sure that spotlight stays on anything that's over the line.

Jedi level

Organize a small team of people who believe in the idea of a values-neutral approach to teaching history and ethnic studies, but make sure that your team represents a broad chunk of the political spectrum: find a mix of Democrats, Republicans, and Independents. Then network with local history or ethnic studies teachers in your local school district and offer to help create lesson plans for them. It's a lot of work planning for lessons, and the odds are good you'll find a teacher who is open to your team's work if you can genuinely show that your team represents a broad range of political affiliations. The existing model ethnic studies framework on the California Department of Education's website has sample lesson plans starting on page 81 of the pdf.

Use that structure to organize your team's efforts.

It's a lot of work putting together a team, doing that networking, and then grinding out draft lesson plans. But you're a Jedi: you can make it happen!

Here's another option: organize a community history symposium to be hosted by your school district. Ensure that a broad range of groups and a broad range of perspectives are represented at the symposium. Your odds of success are probably highest if you first get a commitment to participate in principle from leaders of organizations that represent different constituent communities in your area. For example, where I live on the coast, the local Native American community is Ohlone, and we also have a long history of Portuguese, French, and Mexican folks, among others. In terms of professions, we have a long history of farming, fishing, and art.

Identifying and recruiting people who can represent these various communities and help articulate their local history in a reasonably non-ideological way is your best step one. Then you can approach your school district and make the case for the symposium. Because you'll be able to demonstrate a broad base of community support using the list of people you've already put together, you've got a good shot at getting the symposium off the ground.

Recruit another likeminded Jedi to help you with the organizing. A project like this will be a ton of work. But if you set from the outset a vision of presenting history in as non-ideological a way as possible, in order to make the event as inclusive as possible, then you'll end up creating an event that is far closer to being values-neutral than these things typically are. That's a huge accomplishment! And only a Jedi can make it happen.

* * *

Chapter 10 QR code

History is who we are and why we are the way we are.
– David McCullough

11

Project-Based Learning

Creativity is just connecting things.
- Steve Jobs

* * *

Project-based learning has grown to be an important part of some schools; indeed, a handful of schools have gone exclusively to project-based learning. It can be an incredibly powerful way of engaging students' creativity, and it can get students far more actively involved in their learning process.

A few years ago a middle school in Chicago engaged my team to help them design a custom 4-week project-based learning program featuring a capstone project for their 7th and 8th graders. From the beginning, the vision was that the students would have real agency in the content of the program, so we conducted a brainstorm with the kids and asked them what questions they had about the world. We noted almost a hundred different questions, and then we distilled the questions down to 8 possible classes that would touch on the kids' questions. From there, we worked with the faculty and then with representatives from the 7th and 8th grade classes to develop lesson plans for four courses:

- Sci-Fi Entrepreneurship
- A Brief History of Superheroes
- For The Love of Flavor
- Extreme Creatures

The class I want to discuss here is Sci-Fi Entrepreneurship. A lot of kids get interested in business and technology at relatively young ages, and this class was built for them. In their Science class, the students learned about the science behind near-term technologies such as nanomaterials, genetic editing, and artificial intelligence. In their English class, they read *Ready Player One*, a near-future science fiction novel (it was made into a movie—I highly recommend both the book and the movie). In their Social Studies class, the students learned about the components of a business plan and about how venture capital works. In their Math class, the students learned how to value a company and the math associated with that.

And finally, as a capstone project, the students were put into teams, and each team had to come up with an idea for a business based on one of the near-term technologies. Each team wrote a business plan for their idea, created a valuation model from a simplified template we designed for them, and decided what fraction of their company they were willing to sell for venture capital money and at what valuation. Then the teams got together and we held a "shark tank" event in front of the rest of the school and the parents. It was super fun for the kids, for the teachers, and for the shark tank audience.

As I mentioned in the introduction, in my view students are the most underutilized part of the education system. But here in California, we have a wealth of successful businesses and an immense network of venture capital, and these advantages are *also* underutilized. That's a choice, but we can always start making different choices.

Thus, here's another idea for a pilot project: identify a handful of schools in underserved communities and a core volunteer group of business leaders. Business leaders would put together small venture funds for the schools and serve as investment advisors. Some students would learn the investing side; others would learn entrepreneurship skills and eventually put together business plans to submit for funding. Successful businesses would pay back their initial funding and then after that use profits to bolster the school's student investment fund and fund projects for the school itself. Over time, younger students could grow into the management and investing roles.

Getting a pilot project such as this off the ground would not require any action from the legislature, and it would get our business community more actively engaged in the effort to improve our schools. There are many business leaders who are looking for ways to help our schools; for example, in the Bay Area, Nosterra Ventures[60] has brought together many people looking for ways to have a positive impact. Nonprofits like Junior Achievement[61] have a long history of providing entrepreneurship opportunities for students in underserved communities, and they could play a much bigger role in California.

I personally participated in a Junior Achievement entrepreneurship program when I was in high school; I was elected CEO of our company, and we made over $1,000 selling trivets in just a few months. With the benefit of the internet to market and distribute products, students could very well generate thousands of dollars for their schools, money which could buy equipment for a science lab or instruments for a school band. Students would be gaining valuable experience while helping their school themselves, not waiting for a distant legislature to get around to helping them.

For example, a recent article[62] about the San Francisco Unified School District pointed out that the public school system there did not have junior varsity soccer, despite being considerably larger than the private schools in the city, all of which do offer JV soccer. The article mentions the need to fundraise approximately $45,000 to fund a four-team JV soccer league for the public high schools; this is the kind of project that the students eventually

---

[60] The chapter QR will take you to a link to Nosterra's website. If you live in the Bay Area, I'd encourage you to check out their events.

[61] The chapter QR will take you to the Junior Achievement website. I had a great experience with them as a kid, so I encourage you to check out the work they do!

[62] The chapter QR will take you to a link to the article.

could fund themselves using the profits from their student-run businesses. In addition to all the skills the students would be gaining, they would also gain the sense of pride and independence that would come from knowing they had handled the funding themselves, rather than waiting for money to trickle down from a far-off legislature beholden to its own special interests.

Beyond helping drive more financial resources to under-resourced schools, this initiative would develop entrepreneurial talent in underserved communities. If we ever want to get serious about lifting up our underserved communities, creating stronger economies in them is the fastest, most effective way. And the most durable way to build economies is to foster new businesses in them. Encouraging entrepreneurship and business education for those students who are interested in it will prepare budding entrepreneurs to build new businesses and lift up their communities. And we would be accomplishing that uplift without yet another government program, with its associated bureaucracy and need for permanent taxpayer funding, and therefore without the concomitant fighting that comes with anything in the state budget. Government would be empowering *people* to solve their problems, rather than trying to solve their problems for them.

Finally, one of the most powerful ways we can help prepare our children for an increasingly competitive job market is to build their capacity for integrative thinking across disciplines. School is still primarily an exercise in siloed instruction; math is taught as though it is divorced from all other subjects, history is taught that way, science is taught that way, etc. Yet, the ability to think creatively and integratively across multiple disciplines will very likely be one of the most marketable skills in a flat world brimming with AI-driven tools, and project-based learning offers an excellent opportunity to engage multiple disciplines in a single project in a way that fosters creative, integrative thinking.

This vision of students learning to think creatively and integratively while helping their schools, helping their communities, and helping themselves, all through project-based learning experiences driven by partnerships among schools, business leaders, and nonprofits, is a vision that could powerfully uplift our schools and our communities. It's a vision we can have here in

California, but it would require real leadership at the California Department of Education to drive it. It's up to us as voters to choose that leadership when we get the chance.

How *You* Can Help

There are lots of ways you can support project-based learning in our schools:

Basic level:

Support project-based learning in your local school district by helping source supplies, attending a student showcase, being a judge in a student competition, offering to help identify a guest speaker, or writing a letter of support for project-based learning to your local district Superintendent or school principal.

If you have a business, have a management role in a business, or have the ear of someone in a management role, organize a volunteer group to help mentor student projects or offer your business as a potential field trip for a project team.

Intermediate level:

Embed students in your workplace for "micro-internships" that are tied to their projects. It does take some real time and effort on your part to create an internship that is structured well enough to produce tangible value for the students, but if you do it, you'll get real satisfaction from it.

Work with a school in your area to create an advisory council composed of people from business, STEM, the humanities, and the arts that can work with teachers to brainstorm and design project-based learning opportunities. If the projects, guest speakers, field trips, micro-internship opportunities, capstone events like showcases or competitions, and other details are worked out all from the beginning, the overall effort is more likely to go smoothly and feel successful for all involved.

Jedi level:

Work with a school to create a student investment fund. Help raise some seed capital to get it started. Have a small advisory committee that can work with teachers to help create project-based opportunities with an entrepreneurship component. Consider working with a local Junior Achievement branch or similar organization that can help organize the entrepreneurship angle at the school. Build a team of business leaders who are willing to mentor student businesses over a longer window of time. As profits from student businesses start to flow into the investment fund, recruit business leaders who can serve as investment advisors and help train students in how to select other student business ideas to invest in. Over time, you can create a functioning and self-sustaining entrepreneurship ecosystem. That will take consistent work over several years, so it takes someone with a long-term vision, a good network in business circles, and the willingness to work hard on a project over the long term. In short, it takes a Jedi master. You could be that person!

* * *

Chapter 11 QR code

You have brains in your head.
You have feet in your shoes.
You can steer yourself any direction you choose.
– Dr. Seuss

V

How do we fix the public school system?
Part C: On Innovation

12

Interlude: Wild Geese

Agatha came to me one year midsummer. She needed help preparing for the GMAT, which is the primary test used for applying to top-tier business schools. She needed to go to business school to prepare to take over the reins of a family business.

Reviewing Agatha's background prior to meeting her, she seemed a straightforward case: good undergraduate education, great grades, several years' experience working in investment banking at a top-tier firm. I had her take a diagnostic exam to get her baseline score, as we always do at Advantage Testing, expecting to see the usual investment banking profile: reasonably strong on the quantitative side of the test, spotty on the verbal side of the test.

When the results came back, they were nothing like what I expected: 99th percentile on the verbal section, and... well, let's just say the math score was *low*. In our first meeting, I probed for why that might be, and Agatha revealed that through a combination of sheer determination and clever advocacy, she had managed to avoid taking a single math class since early in high school. When I expressed surprise that she had managed to get a job in investment banking with that background, she said, "I interview well."

That seemed likely; she was clearly very smart and very charismatic. She then revealed that she had survived multiple rounds of layoffs in the aftermath of the dot-com bust because, in her boss's words, "Excel monkeys are a dime a dozen. We can replace them anytime. But no one else here can *write* like you." Note to students: the ability to write well can be a surprisingly valuable asset in the business world.

Having learned all this about Agatha, I smiled and said, "Well, it's time to learn all the math you've been avoiding all these years." And then I slid a very basic Algebra I-based problem across the table to her.

She took one long look at it, looked up at me, and then physically shoved her chair back from the table and got very teary.

I was caught off guard by this; I'd had students cry before – tests can be stressful, a lot of my students are under pressure from home, and young people are often still learning emotional regulation. But I'd never had it happen so *fast*. I tell all my tutors when I train them that 25% of teaching actually winds up being something very akin to therapy, and that was certainly the case here. We talked a lot about her anxiety around math, and at the end of the discussion I offered her a deal: if she would let me push her on the math, then every time it got to feeling like too much, we could take a break for a few minutes and talk about literature and poetry, which we quickly discovered we had a shared interest in.

And that's how we worked together: I saw her for multiple hours every day for six weeks, and at the end of that time, she scored quite well on the GMAT. Along the way, she learned a ton of math, but we also spent a lot of time talking about literature and poetry. Agatha introduced me to the poem "Wild Geese," by Mary Oliver:

Tell me about despair, yours, and I will tell you mine.

For Agatha, that was math. But math calls to us, as Mary Oliver would say, "like the wild geese, harsh and exciting." That's how I positioned math to Agatha, and she learned a lot of it. And then she went on to be very successful.

That was twenty years ago, but I still see Agatha from time to time when I'm in New York. She's married now, and when I saw her last year I got to read a book to her little boy. She likes to remind me of how many times she shoved back from the table, and I like to remind her that she's perfectly capable of doing math. That's the power of teaching: it can take people to places they never thought they could go, and along the way, it can be a powerful force for healing.

13

AI in Education

Technology is a useful servant but a dangerous master.
– Christian Lous Lange, 1921 Nobel Peace Prize laureate

* * *

I have a team that works with public school teachers one-on-one to train them in how to use AI to make themselves more productive and reduce the amount of time they spend on tasks outside the classroom. I often kick off the work, and when I do, I like to confront one of the core concerns a lot of teachers have about AI: is *this thing gonna take my job?*

There are two basic answers to that question, and it's vitally important that you read both before you react. Here they are:

- **Answer 1:** Yes, AI is going to come for your job. But,
- **Answer 2:** AI is going to take jobs in three waves. And as a teacher, you're in a great position, because teaching will be a *third wave* profession.

Here's what I mean by that. Building on the tradition of Alvin Toffler, who wrote the book *The Third Wave*[63], and Steve Case, former CEO of AOL, who wrote *The Third Wave: An Entrepreneur's Vision of the Future*,[64] let's think of jobs as having three dimensions: an intellectual dimension, a physical dimension, and a human interactivity dimension. The intellectual dimension of the job refers to the fraction of the work that occurs primarily because of mental tasks you perform. The physical dimension of the job is the fraction of the work that occurs primarily because of physical tasks you perform. The human interactivity dimension refers to the fraction of your work that requires you to interact with other human beings.

In this framework, some jobs are primarily one-dimensional. For example, if you're someone whose job is writing copy for advertising, or doing basic journalism, or doing basic image processing, within this framework your job is primarily a one-dimensional intellectual job, because it happens almost exclusively in your mind, and the actual performance of the work doesn't require a high degree of interaction with other humans. To be clear, I'm **not** saying your job isn't important or meaningful! But within our framework here, it's a fairly one-dimensional job. And for that reason, AI is already fast swallowing up these jobs. The roughly 10–15% of folks in these jobs who have the right combination of innate talent, ability to adapt to using AI tools, and frankly, luck, will survive, and even thrive. The other 85–90% of these jobs will be gone within the next few years.

Similarly, fashion modeling is a one-dimensional physical job, and it's just a matter of time before 85–90% of those jobs are gone too. Why scour the world for the handful of people who won the genetic lottery and then schlep them and an army of photographers and assistants all over the world doing photo shoots when, by sometime around next Tuesday afternoon,

---

[63] The chapter QR will take you to a link to *The Third Wave*. It's a timeless classic. Toffler is more well-known for his book *Future Shock*, which he wrote ten years earlier and which is also quite good. It's an interesting look at how people thought about the future two generations ago.

[64] The chapter QR will take you to a link to *The Third Wave: An Entrepreneur's Vision of the Future*. I think in very broad terms he makes some pretty good predictions about how technology is permeating and will continue to permeate everyday life.

you'll be able to generate an AI model according to whatever standard of beauty you want, and then place them in whatever AI-generated tableau you want? A handful of supermodels will survive, and celebrities will always have their opportunities, but all the other models and all the other ancillary jobs supporting them will also soon be gone.

The people who will suffer the most in the transition to our AI-powered future are the people whose jobs go in the first wave, because society will not realize yet the magnitude and the speed with which the change is coming, and none of the work necessary to manage such a huge social transition will get done in the first wave. Though I'm generally wired for optimism, in this case my assessment is that there's zero chance our political class will be that forward-thinking about the issue.

The second wave jobs are the two-dimensional jobs. Driving, which a lot of people assumed would be a first wave job, is really a second wave job because it has a physical dimension you cannot escape, and it also requires a high degree of interactivity with other humans and their vehicles. But it isn't, generally speaking, a particularly demanding intellectual task; if you doubt me on that point, next time you're out on the road observe how many people are actively on their phones while driving, the law be damned.

By roughly halfway through the second wave, the number of people impacted by AI will be large enough that our political class will finally begin to deal with the issue in a non-performative way. But they will still drag their feet and resist doing what needs to be done[65] as long as possible, likely until sometime early in the third wave.

That brings us back to teaching. Teaching is a three-dimensional job: it requires a lot of intellectual processing while you're doing it, it has a physical component that you cannot get around (unless everyone is going to do zoom school, and I think we all saw how *that* turned out), and it requires a high degree of human interactivity, most especially with students who have

---

[65] What needs to be done is almost certainly some form of Universal Basic Income- I think Andrew Yang was right about that. Once 80-90% of the jobs are gone from half the industries, what's the alternative? Mass starvation?

learning differences, have special needs, or have experienced trauma.

AI as it exists today, which basically means large language models, cannot now and will not ever be able to do all three dimensions. AI won't be able to truly teach until we develop Artificial General Intelligence (AGI), and we likely won't have that until we develop quantum computing. Those things are coming, but by the time they get here, the earlier iterations of AI will have already eliminated the one- and two-dimensional jobs. Thus, if you're a teacher you can rest easy knowing that AGI won't get here until after all the suffering brought about from the first and second waves forces society to begin the policy transition to our post-AI future. The good news for teachers is, you will be among those who suffer the least in the transition.

What does all this future talk have to do with our school system today? As I said, I have a team that works with teachers to train them one-on-one on how AI can make them more effective, more efficient, and more *powerful* as educators. That's something AI *can* do today. But it won't fundamentally change teaching as a profession, not until we have AGI. In that sense, today's AI is similar to other technologies that people assumed, wrongly, would fundamentally change teaching (MOOCs, Massive Open Online Courses, for example). For an excellent in-depth discussion of why technology has failed to fundamentally change the teaching profession, I highly recommend *Failure to Disrupt*, by Justin Reich.[66]

What we need is leadership that understands that the primary value of AI is to make educators more powerful as educators, and students more powerful as students. We need leadership that can help schools navigate the transition to a world in which students aggressively use AI. And we need leadership that understands that bringing teachers up to speed on AI does not mean sending them to "professional development" seminars delivered by expensive consultants on the taxpayers' dime. Such "trainings," where teachers sit in conference rooms and passively watch presentations, are a waste of both educators' time and taxpayers' dollars, yet that's the strategy

---

[66] The chapter QR will take you to a link for *Failure to Disrupt*, which I highly recommend if you're interested in the intersection of technology and education.

we use in California today.

In contrast, my team works with teachers one-on-one, educator to educator, in an extremely hands-on style; for example, a middle school math teacher would work one-on-one with someone on my team who teaches math and can demonstrate the capabilities and limitations of AI specifically with regard to teaching math (the models have different capabilities and limitations in different domains.) The training is a continuous cycle of discussion, demonstration, and doing, because actually trying it with patient, supportive guidance is the most effective way to learn.

California could train a small army of educators to fan out and be one-on-one trainers of other teachers in their areas. In this way, educators would lift each other up and lead the way to the future that awaits all of us. Or, we can continue to waste time and money having teachers sit in conference rooms watching slideshow presentations while other states lead the way. That's the kind of leadership we're accustomed to in California. But it doesn't have to be that way. We can choose a different path.

And we should.

How *You* Can Help

AI is changing many aspects of our society quickly, and to what extent we allow it to impact our schools is an important question, one that you can get involved in! Here are a few ideas for how:

Basic level:

First, get yourself educated: go onto your district's website and see what policies or guidelines (if any) they have published on the use of AI in the classroom. Check your county Board of Education website as well and see if there is any countywide guidance offered.

Attend any town hall meetings or info sessions sponsored by your district or school that include AI as a discussion topic. Be prepared to speak up and give your perspective on any of the major issues surrounding AI: student privacy/security, bias, accuracy, impact on student learning, etc.

Intermediate level:

If your school or school district has or forms an AI task force or advisory committee, volunteer to be on it. Your perspective will help shape policy!

Do you have anyone in your network who has expertise in AI? Perhaps someone doing research at a university or someone who works in tech and has relevant expertise? Offer to your local school to bring them in as a volunteer consultant to work with the school's teachers or leadership team to offer feedback or ideas on guiding principles for the use of AI in your school.

Jedi level:

Organize a community "AI in Education" conference that brings together school leaders, educators, families, business leaders, and other community leaders to engage in discussions about AI policy in your school district. Possible talks or activities include:

- Presentations of policies in other school districts around the country that have interesting policy ideas or implementations
- Presentation of student outcomes in the district as a prelude to a brainstorming session on ways AI tools might help improve those outcomes
- A discussion of ethical AI use and impacts on student well-being
- Hosting a panel with representatives from local universities and/or tech companies to brainstorm a process for conducting safe experimentation in a controlled environment with AI to test new ideas before rolling them out schoolwide or districtwide.
- Panel discussion on AI evaluation: how will your school or district track whether any new AI processes or initiatives are producing positive outcomes?

As always, organizing a project like this requires a very high level of networking, patience, and grit. You'll need to recruit minions to help you, and you'll have to give them guidance and support. It's a big undertaking, but a Jedi like you can make it happen. So make it happen!

* * *

Chapter 13 QR code

*Our technological powers increase, but the side effects
and potential hazards also escalate.
- Alvin Toffler, "Future Shock"*

14

Standardized Testing

Liberté, Egalité, Mediocrité!

* * *

One thing that I tell all my students is that everyone is Michael Jordan at something: everyone has something they are naturally good at and would become great at with sustained effort. One of life's little journeys is figuring out what it is you're Michael Jordan at. Some people figure out their Michael Jordan thing early, and others figure it out late. Taking standardized tests is my Michael Jordan thing; I took the SAT and the GRE with literally zero preparation and did very well, and I scored very well on the GMAT with a level of preparation that consisted entirely of buying a $3 used book the day before and doing some problems from it for a couple hours.

I say that as a prelude to saying: by definition then, everything else one does is *not* their Michael Jordan thing, which means it's going to take a lot of hard work sustained over time to produce slow and steady gains. For instance, I really enjoy playing basketball, but it's definitely *not* my Michael Jordan thing. I put roughly 25 years of hard work into getting better at it, and I can say with pride that I am now... not terrible. I mean, I'm not *good*, by any stretch of the imagination, but I'm not terrible either. And I worked hard for that.

For most people, standardized test taking is not going to be their Michael Jordan thing, which means it's going to take a lot of hard work sustained over time to produce slow and steady gains. But it can be done; test taking is a skill, just like playing a sport or a musical instrument, and just as with sports and music, there are discrete techniques and drills that can be taught and practiced to produce real improvement over time.

Now, one may ask, "Why bother getting better at taking standardized tests? It's not fun, like sports or music." It turns out there's a large body of research to support the position that standardized tests are useful not just for assessment purposes – that is, not just for determining whether a student does or does not know a particular fact or skill – but also for enhancing the learning process itself. In a 2015 study by Aaron Benjamin and Hal Pashler,[67] the authors note that standardized testing has been shown to "influence learning, memory, and inference, mostly in positive ways." My personal experience is that standardized test prep has been the primary reason why many of my students ever learned core concepts of reading, grammar, and mathematics.

Unfortunately, standardized testing has become a scapegoat, a convenient target for politicians and some school leaders to sacrifice in the name of "equity." It is well known that state assessments and national tests such as the NAEP and the SAT show vastly different overall results when broken down by race. Black and Latino students tend to score quite a bit lower than white or Asian students. For some people, the clever solution to this problem is to label the tests "racist" and just get rid of them.

Let me ask you: if you had a thermometer that told you every day that you were running a pretty bad fever, which of these two actions would you be most likely to choose?

---

[67] The chapter QR will take you to a link to the study. It's important work; standardized tests are easy to demonize and throw under the bus, as they often are, for mostly performative reasons. Although it's a technical paper, the abstract is very approachable and will tell you what you need to know.

1. Declare the thermometer broken, throw it away, and declare publicly that you have made a bold step for your personal health.
2. Recognize that the thermometer is telling you something really important about your underlying personal health and engage in some serious efforts to identify what's wrong so you could fix it.

I assume you would choose option 2, but our political system and the political parts of our education system mostly choose option 1, which is to get rid of standardized testing and claim they've done something bold for "equity." Why? Because the system has a lot of vested interests in it, and it is extremely inconvenient for those interests if the general public starts noticing how badly the system fails so many students. I have no doubt that for some people, getting rid of standardized testing is done with the best of intentions, but on a practical level it serves no purpose but to hide the failures of the system to properly educate every student, regardless of background. What getting rid of standardized testing *doesn't* do is a single thing for "equity"; it just helps ensure that we'll never break out of the mediocrity our school system is mired in. Liberté, Egalité, Mediocrité!

Of course, it's fair to say that the tests aren't perfect; no tool or measurement device is ever perfect. There are ways the tests could be improved, and that leads our discussion to one of the great disappointments of California in the last few years.

In May of 2020, when it became clear that the covid pandemic was not something that was going to be over in a couple months, the University of California announced that it was adopting a "test blind" admissions policy, meaning that they would not consider test scores in their admissions process even if a student chose to submit them. At the time, as part of the announcement of the new policy,[68] the UC system said it would create a new test that "more closely aligns with what we expect incoming students to know to demonstrate their preparedness for UC."

---

[68] The chapter QR will take you to a link to the UC announcement.

However, in November of 2021, the University of California announced[69] that it would not pursue the idea of creating a new test after all, and further, that it would not consider the existing state assessment (the "Smarter Balanced" test) as an acceptable substitute. In making this decision, California squandered a chance to take a real leadership role in education, instead choosing to take the path of performative virtue-signaling by forgoing testing entirely.

The better path, the path of real leadership, was to build a new, dramatically more insightful and useful standardized test, leveraging advances in technology. Such a test would build off tests like the Smarter Balanced test and the MAP,[70] which represent steps in the right direction but which are limited in their designs. The technology now exists to build a standardized test that is capable of both reflecting each student's individual learning journey and differentiating performance at a far more granular level than current tests allow.

Now, in case you're wondering if I have any specific thoughts about how to actually build such a test, I've got great news: I do! In fact, I have a *lot* of thoughts about that. Let's explore how California could revolutionize standardized testing if it had bold, visionary leadership. But first a couple observations:

1. Large language models (LLMs), ChatGPT for example, can substantially accelerate the production of raw/draft test material, thereby dramatically lowering the cost of production. (As a side note, one of the things my team trains teachers to do is take full advantage of LLMs' ability to quickly produce content.) Because the content generation is so much cheaper, you can dramatically expand the range of content areas that a test covers while still keeping production costs manageable.

---

[69] The chapter QR will take you to the January 2021 report to the UC Board of Regents recommending against making a standardized test and to an article about the November 2021 announcement as well.

[70] The MAP test is used in a few thousand school districts around the country. The chapter QR will take you a link to their site if you are interested.

2. Current test designs feature a fixed number of questions in a fixed amount of time. This both limits the ability of students to fully show what they are capable of and limits the ability of the test to differentiate performance. For example, two different students can both score a 1500 on the SAT yet have vastly different knowledge bases and skill levels. I and my team have helped students of a very wide range of knowledge and ability score 1500+ on the SAT. A better test would differentiate students at a much more granular level, and while the SAT's most recent, computer-adaptive iteration is clearly trying to address that on some level, what they've accomplished is baby steps at best.

3. Currently, test takers typically have no agency in how they take standardized tests. They do fixed sections with fixed numbers of questions in a fixed order, none of which they have any influence over.

So here, in broad strokes, are the characteristics of a redesigned test that is possible with today's technology. First, the test would have a fixed amount of time, but not a fixed number of questions. Consequently, the test would have no upper limit on the score that could be attained.

Second, rather than have just a couple content areas, like "math" and "reading comprehension," the test would feature a knowledge web whose entry points are foundational areas like number operations, English grammar, and general science. As work was completed in the foundational areas, other content areas on the knowledge web would become accessible to the test taker. For anyone who has played the computer game "Civilization," in which different advances in knowledge make additional advances in knowledge become available, the content areas would become accessible in a similar fashion. The students would choose for themselves how they wanted to move through the web, and how much of their time they wanted to spend in any given content area.

With this granularity of subject areas, it becomes possible to create an intellectual fingerprint of each student; for example, one student could demonstrate advanced-for-their-age understanding of astronomy, American fiction, and American history, while another student in the same class or grade could demonstrate advanced-for-their-age understanding of biology, Asian history, math, and architecture.

As an analogy, when you look up into the night sky and see the stars, to the naked eye they all look pretty much the same. But each star is unique, and they show a unique fingerprint in what's called their absorption spectra, a graph of what frequencies of light they absorb. Here's the absorption spectra of our sun:[71]

Absorption Spectra of the Sun

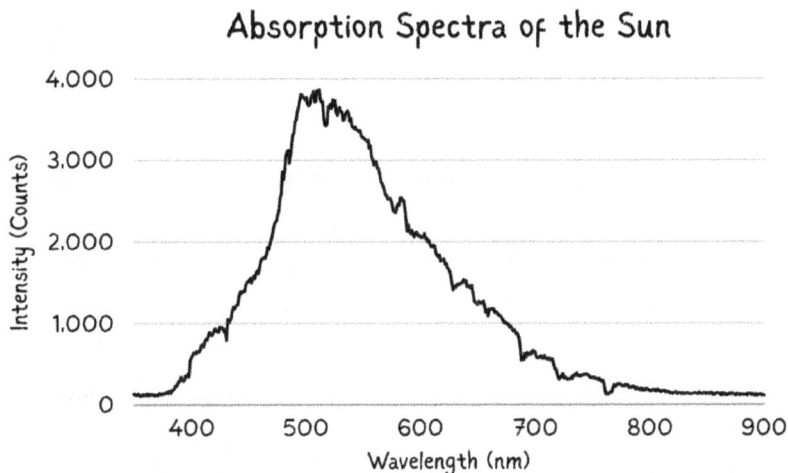

It has a peak around 520 nanometers, which is a wavelength corresponding to green light, though the sun appears reddish to yellowish because of the way light travels through our atmosphere. Now compare that to the absorption spectra for Betelguese, a red giant star that I chose entirely because its name is "Betelgeuse" (pronounced Beetlejuice!):[72]

---

[71] The chapter QR will take you to the site where you can look at a much fancier graph of the sun's spectra. I'll also include the link to Spectroweb, where you can look up the spectra of lots of different stars!

[72] The chapter QR will provide a link to a much fancier graph of Betelgeuse's spectra. By the way, I have no idea what happens if you say its name aloud three times in a row; better safe than sorry has always been my approach.

Absorption Spectra of Betelgeuse

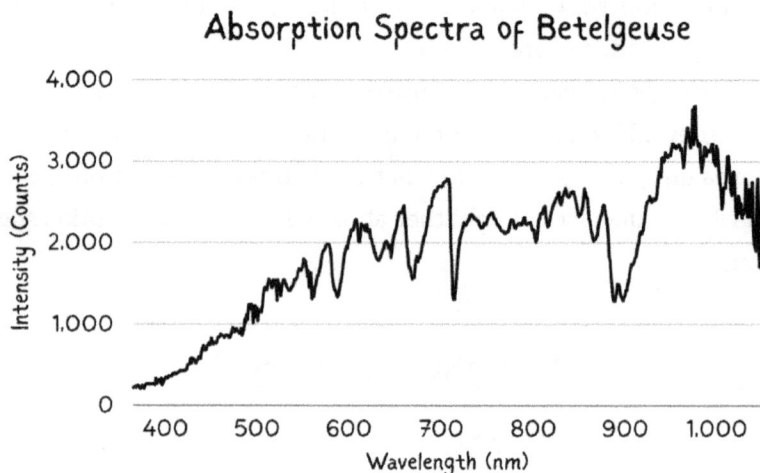

As you can see, Betelgeuse's peaks are in very different places, mostly at higher wavelengths that correspond to red light, which is why Betelgeuse appears very red to us. You get very detailed information about a star from its absorption spectra; it's much more nuanced than "That star is yellow, and that other one is red."

However, with today's standardized tests, you often get information which is literally "that student is yellow" (almost meeting standards), and "that other student is red" (clearly failing to meet standards). That's about it. The California "Smarter Balanced" test just shows you whether you did or didn't meet standards (two buckets that do meet standards, two that don't). It tells you very little about the breadth or depth of a student's knowledge outside of a few content areas.

Here's a sample of the kind of data one could glean from a test of the type I'm describing. This displays results for just a couple key content areas (core skills, Literature, and Math/Computer Science); a much fuller visualization displaying additional content areas (Natural Science, History/Social Studies, Economics/Business, and Art/Music) is on my website.[73]

---

[73] The chapter QR will take you to a much-expanded chart on the website, which is worth looking at to give a fuller sense of what's possible. Because of space limitations on the page, I only included a small fraction of what I put together to illustrate the point.

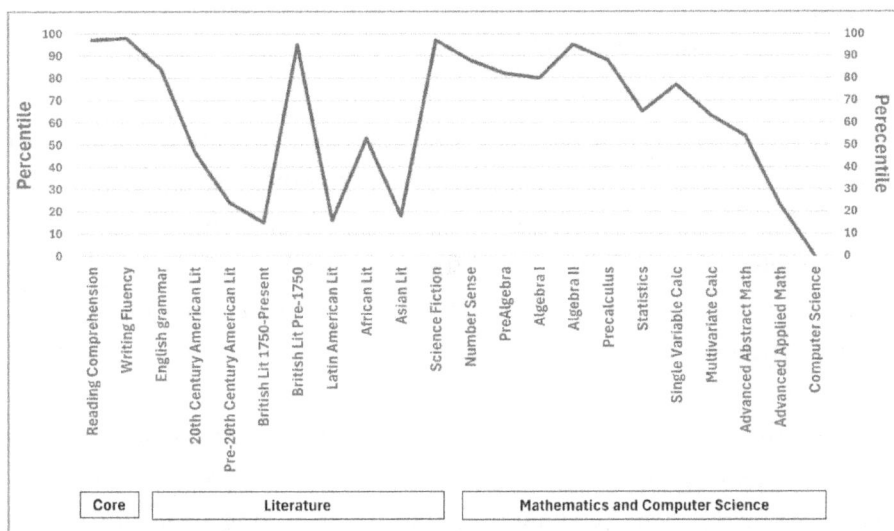

Selected output of a hypothetical "individualized pathway" standardized test

As you can see, this student has strong core skills in reading comprehension and writing and is broadly strong in mathematics, but this student could be encouraged to expand her range of literature beyond her few areas of specialty and could be challenged to take a course in computer science. As a school, you'd have an actionable sense about what academic subjects this student is clearly interested in, where they are performing just fine, and where to encourage or bolster additional instruction. As a potential employer, you'd have a sense that this applicant is a strong generalist.

With this level of insight into a student, colleges or employers would have much more to go on in admissions or hiring decisions, and schools would have more insight into where they could improve their own performance and where they could better support individual students.

Another characteristic of our new test is that it would not have separate reading and writing sections; rather, reading and writing exercises would be embedded in each of the content areas. The way we test reading today is terrible; every kid gets a passage on something like "Trends in Thirteenth Century Florentine Art," and they are expected to read it and answer questions about it. For the microscopic percentage[74] of students who have an interest in Thirteenth Century Florentine art, the exercise will be fun. For everyone else, it's a hard slog through a thoroughly uninteresting passage.

Our new test structure would allow students to mostly read passages related to subject areas they have an actual interest in, since the students are choosing which subject areas to answer questions about, and the scores are calculated based simply on the kinds of text and the skills demonstrated with them. For the narrow purpose of testing whether students can read and comprehend, there is no need to give students passages that are divorced from any academic interest the students actually have.

Given the technology that is now available, our new test would be fully adaptive; that is, getting a question in a content area correct would lead to a slightly more difficult next question. Similarly, getting a question wrong would lead to a slightly easier next question. The smarter balanced test and the MAP test feature a version of this, as does the GMAT (the test to get into business school). The adaptive nature of the test would allow a much more precise assessment of a student's ability level.

The test would also feature an embedded dictionary which would be always accessible; that is, at any time a student could look up any word on the test. Today, tests distinguish between only 2 types of students: those who know a word, and those who do not. But there is tremendous value in differentiating among three types of students: those who know a word, those who don't know a word but are capable of using a reference to acquire the knowledge they need, and those who have neither the ready knowledge nor the skill to acquire that knowledge.

From the test taker's perspective, the benefit of knowing vocabulary is that they wouldn't have to slow down to use the dictionary—remember, there's no upper limit on how many questions you can do or how many points you can score, only a total time limit you can spend on the test. Thus, there's a real benefit to knowing the vocabulary without having to look it up.

---

[74] I presume it's a microscopic percentage, anyway. I concede the possibility that I am the only person in America with functionally zero interest in Thirteenth Century Florentine art.

Similarly, a calculator function would be available at all times above a certain level in the math content area. However, solving questions without using the calculator would add a 25% point bonus. Today, tests only distinguish between students who get questions right and students who get questions wrong. Again, it is useful to distinguish among three types of students: those who have sufficient skill to get a question right without the assistance of a calculator, those who can get a question right only with the assistance of a calculator, and those who can't get a question right at all.

In sum, there's an opportunity to truly *revolutionize* standardized testing, and California could lead the way in that. As a society we do a pretty poor job of identifying and developing the talent we have, especially among lower-income kids. This new test could be a powerful tool in identifying talent at any age, but especially at younger ages and at lower levels of the income spectrum, where so much talent never gets developed.

It's time to get serious about developing our human capital across the entire income spectrum, and revolutionizing standardized testing is just one small part of how we do it. California could be leading the way! But we need leadership at the Department of Education that is willing to push for California to take that leadership role.

How *You* Can Help

There are two primary ways you can be supportive of thoughtful, well-designed standardized testing policies and help California break out of its *A is for Average* mentality: first, by ensuring that there is a clear narrative explaining their benefits, so that the voices that would try to eliminate them don't dominate the discussion, and second, by helping create momentum to bring standardized testing back to the University of California's admissions process.

Basic level:

Understand what the test scores look like for your school and your district.

The chapter QR will take you to my website, where I'll show you how to look these numbers up. Understand the breakdown of the numbers by race; remember, California politicians never miss a chance to pat themselves on the back for their commitment to "equity." Do the numbers suggest they should be patting themselves on the back?

Share a fact sheet on standardized testing with friends, neighbors, and parents in your school district. The chapter QR will take you to a fact sheet on my website, but you can make your own if you prefer.

Intermediate level:

Write an op-ed or a blog post explaining why you think standardized testing has value and should be retained as part of a data-driven system of accountability.

Organize a "test day" support program for the kids at your local school. Partner with local businesses to provide things like healthy breakfasts or treats for when the kids have finished their testing.

Jedi level:

Help ratchet up the level of pressure on the University of California system. The UC system has a Board of Regents that holds public meetings. Organize 1–2 people to give a public comment on the positive impact that standardized testing had on their lives. For example, as a low-income kid whose parents couldn't afford fancy extracurriculars, I got on the radar of a school like Pomona College in part because of my SAT scores. There are lots of other folks like me out there who can speak to that! Find a mix of people by race, income level, and so forth, and only have 1–2 people give a comment at any one meeting, so you can have fresh faces at the next meeting. If other Jedi around the state also do this, we'll build quite a pressure campaign. Getting the UC system to change course would truly be Jedi level!

* * *

Chapter 14 QR code

Standardized admissions tests have proved especially good at predicting performance of black college applicants.
– The Wall Street Journal, in an article about the University of Texas's decision to reinstate standardized testing in admissions

VI

How do we fix the public school system?
Part D: On Opportunity

15

Interlude: Los Ricos También Lloran

("The Rich Also Weep," a classic telenovela)

* * *

The headquarters of Advantage Testing are in New York City. During the four years I worked in NYC, the central office team eventually began calling me "The Wolf" after the character in Pulp Fiction whom one called if one had an impossible situation that needed cleaning up.

One day in 2010, a few years after I'd moved to the Bay Area and founded Advantage Testing there, I got a call from HQ. A student, Ashley, was a first-year student in a top-tier business school and was in the midst of the intro class for Accounting. It was a ten-week class, and at the five-week point they'd had a midterm exam. Ashley had scored 10 out of 100 points on the exam, and she had called the NYC office to request someone who could work with her remotely, 2–3 hours every day, to catch her up and prepare her for the final, which she would need to ace.

There aren't a lot of people within Advantage who can tutor something as specialized as Accounting, and back in 2010 there weren't a lot of tutors who regularly worked remotely with students. Skype was about the only tool for remote work back then. And 2–3 hours per day, every day, was a big ask from a bandwidth perspective. HQ spent a few days trying to get someone in NYC to handle the case, and no one felt they could.

So they called The Wolf.

By the time all the arrangements were done and Ashley was officially on my plate, she was about to enter week seven of the ten-week class. I had three and a half weeks to teach her ten weeks of material. So we booked our first lesson, and after the usual icebreaker conversation, I asked her just about the most basic question one could ask an accounting student: if I sell ten widgets for five dollars apiece, what do I debit, and what do I credit?

Ashley immediately melted down completely.

This was not being stoically teary-eyed, like Agatha in the Wild Geese interlude. This was worthy of a telenovela: it was loud, and it was *dramatic*. And it went on for a while. I did my best to patiently and empathetically guide her back to a place where we could get started on accounting, and when it seemed we were there, I again asked that basic question, which is the accounting equivalent of "What is ten times five?"

Again, Ashley immediately melted down completely.

This second meltdown actually topped the first one in both duration and intensity. Again I patiently and empathetically guided her back to a place where we could get started, and again I asked that basic question.

And she melted down again.

By the time I'd talked her down from the ledge a third time, we were almost an hour into our lesson, and we had yet to accomplish *anything.* Knowing what was coming, I asked my basic question one more time, and this time when she melted down, I tried a different approach:

Gus: "Hey, real quick, I just want to say, it's totally okay for you to have these feelings, and I want to give you some space for them, but I'm really hungry, so I'm going to go to the kitchen and make some toast."

Ashley [looking shocked]: "Wait, what?"

Gus: "No, seriously, take all the time you need! But I'm going to go make myself some food."

And then I got up and walked away.

When I came back five minutes later, toast and OJ in hand, and repeated my basic question, Ashley hesitantly gave me a mostly correct answer. And that was our breakthrough moment. From then on, any time Ashley resorted to histrionics, I would offer one minute of patience and empathy, and if she didn't get herself under control by then, I would just tell her to take all the time she needed, and I would get up and walk away. Once she saw that histrionics accomplished nothing, and that I would calmly and implacably always return us to the subject at hand, she began resorting to histrionics less and less.

In time, it became clear that Ashley had a pretty quantitative mind, and after three and a half weeks of intensive work, she did, in fact, ace her accounting final. She went on to do very well in business school, and her first job out of school was in a finance role with a small company. I attended her graduation, and I was proud to see how far she'd come.

Here's why I wanted to share this story: I grew up in the seventies and eighties, when the reaction to pretty much everything was, "Walk it off!" There are plenty of times when that is a terrible way to react. But our cultural pendulum has swung so far in the opposite direction that now it's as if it's a failure or a grave injustice if a kid feels even a moment of negative emotion. But true learning will necessarily involve at least some struggle, suffering, and frustration. And it's good that it does! Only by experiencing these things will kids learn the toughness and resilience they will need to thrive in a world which is beautiful in many ways, but which is also at times incredibly harsh and unforgiving. A great learning experience leaves kids not just with knowledge, but also with greater toughness and resilience.

16

School Choice

*The goal should be to give every child, of any skin color,
the equal opportunity to develop in the way that suits them best.*
– Magatte Wade

* * *

In the preface, I told the story of how I was the only one of my neighborhood friends to graduate from high school. While all of my friends went to Roosevelt High School, which had a 25% graduation rate, I was fortunate enough to go to a private high school. To achieve that, my parents rented out half our house and saved up for my tuition.

All of that effort was to create an opportunity to exercise a small degree of school choice and avoid a generationally failing public school. Thus, dear reader, it is time for me to confront you with a hard, uncomfortable truth: everyone above a certain income level *already has* school choice. They exercise that choice in one of two ways:

1. Move to an area with great public schools.
2. Pay to send their kids to private school.

Option 1: Move to an area with great public schools.

This is typically the more expensive option. My parents, for instance, could not afford this option. In 2007, I opened my first Advantage Testing office in Palo Alto, which has excellent public schools at every level. One of the first calls I received was from a local mom looking for tutoring for her son.

I walked her through our program and approach and she sounded quite enthusiastic. Then, the conversation turned to our rates. When I told her, there was a brief silence before she erupted: "Why do you think I paid millions of dollars to live in this TINY house in Palo Alto? So that I wouldn't have to pay a fortune for education!"

And then she hung up on me.

You see, the demand for excellent public schools vastly exceeds the supply of excellent public schools, and so neighborhoods with excellent public schools quickly become very expensive places to live. Yet people with kids and with the required level of income will choose to "pay millions of dollars to live in this tiny house" if it means access to a quality public school. Of course, people without that level of income cannot make that choice; my parents certainly could not. That leaves:

Option 2: Pay to send their kids to private school.

With long-range planning and careful saving and three full-time jobs between them, my parents made this choice. And because they did, my siblings and I all went to good private high schools, got decent educations, and because of that went on to have better lives than our parents did.

Option 2 doesn't require the level of income that option 1 does, but not everyone can afford option 2 either. In the low-income neighborhood I grew up in, most people couldn't afford either option. And so, with no other choice, they sent their kids to Roosevelt, knowing that it would be a miracle if their kids got through it. And most didn't—either they dropped out rather than continue to spend time in a failing school, or they got caught up in the juvenile justice system.

If you've never lived in such an area, then you likely have no real idea what a failing public school does to a neighborhood. You likely have no real idea what it communicates to the families and children of that neighborhood that they will be sentenced to go to a failing school whether they like it or not. You likely do not understand the message it sends to those families and those children about how much society actually values them, and no number of pretty speeches about "equity" and "equity priority communities" and "our commitment to public education" will ever paper over the gaping hole that a failing public school punches in the heart of a community.

And that brings me to school choice.

The first thing you should understand about school choice is that it can mean a lot of different things, but most people only think of one particular thing when they hear the words "school choice": vouchers. It's analogous to universal healthcare: there are actually many different ways to achieve universal healthcare – England's model (the government owns everything) is different from Switzerland's (basically Obamacare), which is different from Singapore's (universal health savings accounts). But mention universal healthcare in the United States, and almost everyone just assumes you're talking about "Medicare for All," even though there are many other options.

Similarly, almost everyone immediately thinks of vouchers when they hear the words "school choice," but there are many different school choice policies. EdChoice[75] has a pretty comprehensive list of options and what they mean. This book is focused on how to solve the two-tiered educational outcomes that California's existing public school system produces, so we will focus on the four options most likely to move the needle on that: public charter schools, magnet schools, open enrollment, and microschools. The two choice options that people are most likely to have heard of, vouchers and homeschooling, we're not going to spend as much time on. But since vouchers and homeschooling tend to be the first things anyone thinks of when they hear the words "school choice," let's talk briefly about them.

---

[75] The chapter QR will take you to the EdChoice page with their list of school choice options and their definitions, which I've summarized here.

Vouchers

If you don't know what a voucher system is, the way it works is that the per-student amount of money that the government would normally spend to fund a public school goes to the student instead of the school, and then the student can spend that money as tuition at any school they want, public or private. The reason we're not going to focus on vouchers in this book is that there's no solid evidence that vouchers lead to any improvement in the public school system. Vouchers do, by definition, provide more choice for families, and they at least sometimes succeed in rescuing some kids from failing public schools. But they do not appear to have any meaningful impact on the performance of traditional public schools. This is in stark contrast to public charter schools, for which there IS substantial evidence that they lead to improvements in the performance of traditional public schools. Since improving public schools is the focus of this book, we will leave vouchers for others to discuss more fully.

Homeschooling

Homeschooling can be an incredible gift that parents give a child, *provided* they are willing to do the incredible amount of work it takes to execute homeschooling well. My team and I have worked with many homeschooling families over the years, designing custom curricula for them to accomplish their educational goals for their children. It's incredibly creative and rewarding. But it is a *lot* of work. As with vouchers, much has been written about homeschooling, and since homeschooling is outside the public school system and is not realistically a viable strategy for improving the public school system itself, it's out of scope for this book.

Let's turn to the school choice options that exist *within* the public school system and consider how they might benefit families and/or traditional public schools: public charter schools, magnet schools, open enrollment, and microschools.

Public Charters

The first thing to understand about public charter schools is that they are *public schools.* I mention this because one of the immediate objections to any discussion of charter schools is that they "just take resources away from public schools." In a district whose schools are already performing well, that's an argument that perhaps can be made in good faith. But in a district like the one I grew up in, where Roosevelt High School put up a 25-year record of having a roughly 25% graduation rate, that is not a good faith argument. No family in my neighborhood would ever send their kids to Roosevelt if they had another option. Charter schools provide such an option, while still remaining true to America's commitment to providing universal public education.

Another frequent objection is that many charter schools fail. Perhaps, but if you went around my old neighborhood in South St. Louis and offered the families there a choice between sending their kids to a new public charter school with a 50-50 chance of delivering a quality education and sending them to Roosevelt High, which had functionally zero chance of delivering a quality education, I think you'd find that pretty much everyone would take the 50-50 shot.

The fact is, there's a large and growing body of evidence to suggest that public charter schools *do* increase educational outcomes, and their impact is the biggest on low-income, minority students in urban areas. For California, where so many of the most struggling districts are in cities like Los Angeles, San Francisco, and Oakland, the failure to implement more public charters in struggling districts represents a colossal waste of an opportunity, a waste which falls hardest on primarily low-income, overwhelmingly Black and brown kids. California has the world's 4th largest economy, and a tech sector that all but prints money, but perhaps the richest thing in all of California is the irony of seeing a state that never misses an opportunity to pat itself on the back for its commitment to "equity" deliberately withhold or slow walk the one thing that has ever proven capable of closing the black–white achievement gap: public charter schools.

If you'd like to read a good book on the impact that charter schools can have, I strongly recommend *Charter School City*,[76] by Douglas Harris. In the aftermath of Hurricane Katrina, the city of New Orleans converted its entire school system to charters. Since then, students in that system have made gains on essentially every dimension: state assessments, the ACT, the high school graduation rate, and the college enrollment rate. In most cases, the size of the improvement was substantial; for instance, the college enrollment rate for New Orleans public school graduates went from 60th in the state of Louisiana up to 10th. And the results neatly dispense with one of the common forms of pushback on charters, which is that they skim off the most talented and motivated students. That cannot be the case in New Orleans, where the entire system was converted to charters.

Even in districts where not all public schools have been converted to charter schools, there is a large and growing body of evidence that suggests that the addition of a public charter school to the ecosystem raises the performance of the traditional public schools in the same district. For example, a study by Sarah Cordes of Temple University[77] showed that "charter schools significantly increase TPS [traditional public school] student performance in both English Language Arts and math, and decrease the probability of grade retention. Effects increase with charter school proximity and are largest in TPSs co-located with charter schools."

It's worth asking the question: why do charter public schools so often perform better than traditional public schools? Remember: the traditional public school system delivers the results it is perfectly designed to produce. To work in the traditional public school system is to work in an environment with an enormous number of rules and constraints on your freedom of action, your freedom to *teach*. An important advantage that charters bring to the table is simply that they are much less constrained in what they can do, which gives them the freedom to more creatively and effectively solve the problem of improving student outcomes. And because teachers are less constrained in

---

[76] The chapter QR will take you to the link to *Charter School City*. It's a really good read; I highly recommend it.

[77] The chapter QR will take you to a link to the study.

how they work, and the school has fewer regulations it has to comply with, the school needs less administration, which means more resources are put toward actually educating the students.

So what's the solve? Here again, a Superintendent could have real influence by working with Local Educational Agencies, County School Boards, the California Commission on Charter Schools, and the general public to expand the number of charter schools in struggling districts. Note that the effort would be on <u>struggling</u> districts; districts where the schools are already well-performing and parents already have good choices are not the places to prioritize adding charter public schools.

To be clear, public charter schools are not a magic bullet. They don't always work, and they often have more complex relationships with unions because they are not beholden to the same set of rules as traditional public schools. But they are an important tool in the toolbox, and when a neighborhood public school has been struggling for a long time, then if we truly care about the families in that neighborhood all the options need to be on the table.

Magnet Schools

If you're not familiar with the term, a magnet school is a public school where the curriculum is specialized in some way. For instance, some magnet schools are for gifted and talented kids generally. Some are focused on Science and Technology, like Bronx Science in New York City. Others are focused on career technical education, with curricula that educate students in fields such as agriculture or animal husbandry. Their specialization often allows them to draw students from a much wider geographic area than a traditional neighborhood public school.

For instance, I graduated 8th grade from a magnet school in St. Louis called Enright Classical Junior Academy (CJA). I was bused to that school from my neighborhood on the South Side of St. Louis. CJA supported gifted and talented kids from across the city and was very well integrated in a city that was and still is very racially segregated.

SEVENTH GRADE

Pro tip: Do not show up to a 1980s-era middle school looking anything like this. There are consequences.

Being in a school that pushed kids to develop more quickly by identifying and grouping a gifted subset was a breath of fresh air after my neighborhood elementary school, which was similar in racial diversity to CJA but completely different in average ability level. I enjoyed school far more and learned far more than if I had stayed at the neighborhood school.

Here in California, the state does offer nominal support for Gifted and Talented Education (GATE) programs, but the state office largely washes its hands of it, and local districts are left to figure everything out on their own about how to deliver services, what services to deliver, and whom to deliver the services to. While local control is indeed a good organizing philosophy, there's a difference between local control without state support and local control with it. Also, California is one of only a few states that make no attempt to systematically identify gifted and talented students. In my view, this state of affairs is reflective of a pervasive mentality within the leadership at the California Department of Education that views gifted and talented education as fundamentally "inequitable". It's the same *A is for Average* mentality that caused people to take Algebra I out of middle school and that caused the Palo Alto public school system to get rid of honors Biology and lump everyone together, regardless of ability or interest.

That kind of undifferentiated approach is certainly one form of "equity," but it's deeply misguided. It's just a matter of time before someone tries to argue that we should just merge the varsity and JV teams together, because it's unfair to the JV kids to be separated from the varsity kids because of something as simple as athletic ability or level of development. And if a couple of the kids have Division I or professional level ability, well, we shouldn't coach them any differently from the kids who will never play the sport past high school—it would be unfair!

The reality is, a school system that was truly equitable would educate each student as closely as possible to their full potential, recognizing that students have an enormous range of potential. An equitable system would not pretend that all kids have the same potential or the same needs, and it would not structure its curriculum that way.

What California needs is a reinvigoration of its approach to gifted and talented education. It should start by systematically identifying gifted and talented potential early. As we discussed in Chapter 14, California could develop a standardized testing mechanism that could be used to do that. We should also be identifying a broader range of giftedness; as we'll discuss in the next chapter, kids should get early exposure to the foundations of career technical education: exposure to industrial arts, home economics, and where possible, agricultural trades. Some students have amazing gifts in these areas, and trying to force them onto a traditional college-bound track is not necessarily in their best interest.

California should look at ways to expand its magnet schools; indeed, in areas where enrollment is declining, magnet programs that draw students from a wider area may be one way to help manage an otherwise painful demographic transition. But being serious about expanding magnet schools and identifying gifted and talented kids would require leadership at the California Department of Education that is not beholden to a perspective that achieves "equity" by removing opportunities from kids who would truly benefit from them.

Open Enrollment

Open enrollment policies vary widely, but the core idea is that students are allowed to enroll in a school outside their neighborhood public school. Some districts, such as Los Angeles Unified, have an open enrollment policy which allows students who are already within the LA Unified system to apply to any grade-appropriate school within the district. Other districts allow students from outside the district to attend. This is most commonly done through the "District of Choice" program, which is a program that districts can opt into if they choose. Participating districts designate a certain number of seats as available to students from outside the district.

Open enrollment was once coordinated through the California Department of Education, but similar to the approach with gifted and talented students, everything has been kicked to the local level, and the state's role has been reduced to "notify us if you decide to participate". Again, while I am philosophically an enthusiastic supporter of local control in government policy, not very many districts actually participate in the Districts of Choice program, and state leadership in articulating the case for doing so is notably lacking. California needs leadership at the Department of Education that is enthusiastic about increasing the number of choices for families whose kids are stuck in subpar schools, and given the number of those students and the number of higher-performing schools that face enrollment declines, there's a huge opportunity that is being missed—an opportunity to increase choice for families, address declining enrollment in higher-performing schools by bringing in more students, and thereby increase the aggregate quality of education that our students receive. But that opportunity will remain a missed opportunity unless and until we choose the kind of leadership that will be a force for increasing choices for families.

Microschools

Microschools support a handful of students at a time, often with a highly customized curriculum. They can be either public or private, though in practice most are private. My team had long specialized in developing custom curricula, but when COVID-19 hit, we had to dramatically scale up our capacity, because we were inundated with requests for pod classes; i.e., microschool classes. Using a model of interviewing the kids in each pod to identify their interests, we developed custom classes that touched on the questions the kids had about the world. Here are just a few of the pods we developed:

- Capital Markets for Tweens
- The Biology of My Pet
- Brilliant Minds: Scientists Who Shaped Our World
- Drawing Nature
- An Introduction to the Bible as Literature
- I Have No Mouth and I Must Scream: An Introduction to Science Fiction
- Famous Last Words

Microschools allow for this level of customization, and for families willing to do the consistent, time-intensive work of sourcing curricula, they can provide a deep and rich learning experience. For that reason, California should enthusiastically support microschools as an option for those families who are willing to put in the tremendous amount of effort it takes to make them work well (and it really does take a tremendous amount of effort to make them work well, if you're thinking about a microschool as an option). As of this writing, it does not appear that the California Department of Education has anyone dedicated to providing support for microschools; whether this neglect is benign or not, new leadership at the Department could establish dedicated support for microschools, and when we next choose the leadership of the Department, we should look for someone who would create that support.

In conclusion, don't fall into the trap of thinking that any discussion of "school choice" is necessarily an assault on the public school system. Public charters, magnet schools, and open enrollment are part of the public school system, and even microschools can exist within the public school system if people choose to do them that way. What these policies represent is simply a way to give families more options for their kids' education, and that is especially important for families who otherwise will face the prospect of sending their kids to a school like the one I grew up around, a school that failed an entire generation of kids. We have an opportunity to choose leadership that recognizes this, and it's vital that we do, so that we don't fail another generation of mostly low-income kids here in California.

How *You* Can Help

There are lots of ways you can get involved in the issue of increasing the range of choices that families have in educating their kids:

Basic level:

Follow at least one education policy organization on social media. Examples include the California Policy Center, EdChoice, Fordham, and Heritage.

Go to your school district's website and learn what their policy is on transfers, magnet schools, and charter schools.

Subscribe to a newsletter on education policy. Set a goal of reading at least one article per week. Send any articles you find particularly interesting to friends and family. They are more likely to read such an article if it comes from you, and because of that, you'll be helping to educate the general public on education policy.

You are represented by a State Assemblymember, a State Senator, a member of Congress, and two U.S. senators. Who are they? What are their positions on school choice?

Intermediate level:

Volunteer with a charter school in your area, or volunteer with a school choice advocacy group. It may take a few tries to figure out what the best tasks or projects for you to help out on are, but hang in there – there's always a role for you, and volunteering is incredibly meaningful.

Volunteer on one or more campaigns of candidates who believe in offering more choices to families. Volunteers are the lifeblood of campaigns. Candidates vary widely in how effective they are at harnessing the energy of volunteers, so even if it doesn't work out particularly well with one candidate, you can find another easily.

Jedi level:

Organize a lobby day where you take a group of constituents to Sacramento to lobby your state Assemblymember and/or your State Senator. Be realistic: if this is your first time organizing such an event, you're probably not going to get a meeting with your Assemblymember or Senator directly; you'll get a meeting with a staffer. But start with that. The more people you organize, the better, and the more diverse they are, the better. You want a mix of income levels and racial backgrounds, and you want some people who can tell a good story about how school choice benefited them, or about how the lack of choice is hurting their kids. People respond most strongly to narratives, so having some people who can tell a good, brief story is key.

Try to see as many legislators as you can, but always start with the ones who directly represent you. Then you can branch out to the ones who are on the Education committees in the Assembly and Senate. If you can build a big enough following or organize an event every year, you'll stand a better shot at eventually getting a meeting with your actual representatives. Organizing a lobby day is a ton of work, but you're a Jedi – you got this!

* * *

Chapter 16 QR code

More than 50 years have passed since Gov. George Wallace was forced to allow black students to walk into public schools, but today many of these very same schools are failing. It is long past time to provide the children trapped in these schools with access to something better by embracing school choice, by creating more options and by supporting more educational opportunities throughout the country.

– Kevin P. Chavous, former D.C. Council member and education advocate

17

Career Technical Education

Far and away the best prize that life offers
is the chance to work hard at work worth doing.
– Theodore Roosevelt

* * *

I am fortunate to have grown up in a family where my siblings and I have remained close over the years. My younger sister manages a hospital system in Houston. My younger brother Mike is a seriously lethal former special forces Marine. After picking up a Purple Heart in Iraq, he came home to the U.S. and taught Urban Counterinsurgency Techniques at Camp Pendleton, so he also has the gift of teaching.

And then there's my youngest brother, Will. It's entirely possible he's the smartest of the four of us, but you could never tell that based on his school records. It took several schools and some extra time to get him through high school; he had a tendency to do an assignment, be satisfied that he had proven to himself that he could do it, and then never turn it in. He was manifestly uninterested in any kind of external validation, especially grades or test scores.

He spent a lot of time with my grandpa, whom you read about earlier in this book. Grandpa had served in the Air Force in World War II, had seen a lot of the world, and was good with his hands: he was a carpenter and a plumber. Will inherited that same gift of being able to work well with his hands, but he didn't really have an opportunity to explore that until he joined the Air Force.

In the Air Force, Will discovered that his ability to work with his hands, plus his raw intelligence, plus a gift for understanding what makes machines tick, made him an excellent mechanic for our most advanced fighter jets. He spent 20 years in the Air Force, served several tours in the Middle East, traveled the world, and fixed a lot of very expensive planes. Though he's retired from the Air Force, he's still somewhere in the Middle East (he's like an outdoor cat; you never really know where he is until he turns up) continuing to fix our military's planes as a contractor. He's had a great career, because he finally found his Michael Jordan thing, which is fixing complicated machines.

I told you Will's story because it's a shame the school system didn't identify his gifts earlier. He was on the same conveyor belt everyone else was on: he was expected to get good grades, get into a good college, and find a nice white-collar job. But that wasn't who he was, and he almost certainly would have had a very different experience in school had the school system made any effort to identify students like him and offer a pathway more appropriate to his interests.

In California, our two-tiered outcome problem is mirrored in how districts approach career technical education (CTE), which is the term used to describe education that prepares students to pursue careers in various trades. We've allowed CTE to become something that students of higher-income districts have little to no contact with, while at the same time we actively promote it to students of lower-income districts, where reading and math scores suggest that we've given up on the idea of providing them a traditional education even remotely comparable to what the kids in the higher-income districts get. This state of affairs is a disservice to both populations of students; higher-income students all get pressured to follow a college-bound track, even if they might have a gift for a trade and would be happy pursuing it, while lower-income students are pushed toward trades, very likely leaving lots of undeveloped smartness on the table. And as we discussed in Chapter 1, leaving smartness on the table negatively impacts the standard of living for all of us.

In recent years, CTE in California is a good news/bad news story: the good news is that enough people have realized that we need to be doing a lot better on the CTE front that the California state legislature has finally made some real investments in it. The bad news is that those investments have been made in a highly fragmented way (split up among such programs as CTE Incentive Grants, the Strong Workforce Program, and the Golden State Pathways Program) without any coherent plan to guide that spending. We know there's no coherent plan, because in 2023 Governor Newsom signed an executive order to create one: the "Master Plan on Career Education."[78] Spending hundreds of millions of dollars for several years and only afterward deciding that maybe there should be some kind of plan to guide the spending is peak California.

Now that the rapidly changing landscape of employment has generated some urgency, and planning for CTE is taking place in earnest, we can talk about what we should be doing differently. Here are a few ideas:

First, CTE courses should be <u>required</u> in middle school. The California Department of Education lists fifteen different industry sectors for CTE, with multiple pathways within each sector:

1. Agriculture and Natural Resources
2. Arts, Media, and Entertainment
3. Building and Construction Trades
4. Business and Finance
5. Education, Child Development, and Family Services
6. Energy, Environment, and Utilities
7. Engineering and Architecture
8. Fashion and Interior Design
9. Health Science and Medical Technology
10. Hospitality, Tourism, and Recreation
11. Information and Communication Technologies
12. Manufacturing and Product Development

---

[78] The chapter QR will take you to a link to the current Master Plan for Career Education.

13. Marketing Sales and Services
14. Public Services
15. Transportation

Students should be required to take one CTE course each semester in 6th through 8th grade, coming from at least three different industry sectors. This policy will ensure that all students get at least some real exposure to CTE.

Second, all CTE courses at the high school level should have open enrollment for all students in California. Although in practice very few students are likely to come from very far away, students wanting to pursue a particular variant of CTE should be able to do so, even if it means spending some time at a different school from their regular high school.[79]

Third, we need to get serious as a state about setting up apprenticeship programs, starting in high school and continuing through college. Part of that has to happen through the legislature, to make it as easy as possible for companies, particularly small businesses, to set up apprenticeships.

Fourth, we need to work with regional industries to create models for what successful apprenticeships look like, particularly for smaller businesses. Many businesses may well be interested in having apprenticeships but may not know how to actually implement them well, and providing that support will be critical.

Fifth, planning efforts need to include representatives from a wide range of industries, so that CTE plans and programs are in alignment with the changing needs of employers. The first time I ever attended a public event for my representative in the state legislature, he detailed his ongoing, multiyear effort to make computer science a requirement in high school. By the time the legislature gets around to actually doing that, AI will have eviscerated most of the jobs that might once have justified this initiative. The reality is that government will never be able to keep up with an accelerating rate of change in private sector employment needs, so the correct thing to do is for

---

[79] Of course, schools should still be allowed to give priority to their own students and should be reimbursed for cross-enrolled CTE students.

the legislature to create and support processes that allow for more regional and local planning in conjunction with industry. Only then will CTE programs have a chance to keep up with the changing needs of employers.

Sixth, we need to have robust, transparent data on CTE at all levels so that we can track what's happening and identify areas to improve. The data situation for CTE is not unlike what it is for teacher hiring and retention: what data exists is fragmented and not particularly transparent.

Implementing a robust system of CTE will require coordination among the K–12 education system, our higher education system, all levels of government, and the private sector. But since the K–12 education system is the origin point for the workforce, it's particularly important that the leadership of the K–12 system be extremely active and engaged in driving the collective effort. With the right leadership, we can finally get serious about creating a CTE system that offers kids like my brother Will a meaningful path to rewarding employment in whatever industry or trade best fits them, regardless of their income level. That's a goal we should be pursuing relentlessly.

How *You* Can Help

Here are some ways you can get involved in the development of career technical education for our kids:

Basic level:

Offer a job shadow half-day for one or more high school students at your place of employment. Coordinate with your local public school to get sign-ups. Or host a 60–90 minute field trip by a class of middle school or high school students.

If your local school district is applying for a grant from one of the many state programs involved in CTE (CTE Incentive Grants, the Strong Workforce Program, the Golden State Pathways Program, etc.), write a brief letter of support for the application. I serve on the Citizens Advisory Committee for a government agency that doles out hundreds of millions of dollars in grant funds (the San Mateo County Transportation Authority), and I can tell you that clear evidence of deep public support for an application goes a very long way.

Intermediate level:

Coordinate with a local public school and with your own network to crowd-source a makerspace at the school. Work with school officials to see what space is available, and then brainstorm what types of materials and supplies would be best given the expertise of the teaching staff. Then use your network to make the funding and the materials happen.

Set up a microinternship (20–40 hours) at your place of employment to run during a school break. Define one clear project that could be completed by a young person in that time and identify one person to own mentoring and guiding the student toward completion of the project.

Coordinate a sector event at your local school, either during the schoolday or one evening. Use your professional network to source a representative from several different companies in your industry sector, and offer each representative five minutes to talk about their company and the opportunities for careers there, particularly for young people. In addition to being great for the kids, it's an opportunity for you to do some networking in your industry, which never hurts.

Jedi level:

Help found a registered youth apprenticeship with the California Division of Apprenticeship Standards.[80] The Division's website has detailed instructions for how to set up an apprenticeship. Among other things, you'll need to set up a commitment of a certain number of paid hours, a training plan, and structured mentorship. But California's kids desperately need more of these

---

[80] The chapter QR will take you to a link to the Division of Apprenticeship Standards website.

apprenticeships; this is Jedi-level work!

Fundraise to endow a teacher fellowship, most likely a paid summer externship and/or professional development, that places a CTE instructor with a company so the instructor can keep their skills and their course content up-to-date with industry trends and needs.

Do you have skills in one of the CTE industry sectors? Become a CTE instructor of record. You'll need to get a Designated Subjects Teaching Credential.[81] But once you have it, you can start sharing your knowledge with the next generation. Pass on the wisdom and experience you've gained in your career; there's nothing more Jedi level than that!

* * *

---

[81] The chapter QR will take you to the website detailing the process for gaining the credential.

Chapter 17 QR code

Seest thou a man diligent in his business?
He shall stand before kings; he shall not stand before mean men.
— Proverbs 22:29

18

Higher Education

May the odds be ever in your favor.
– Caesar Flickerman (The Hunger Games)

* * *

On March 12th, 2019, the news broke that several families had paid enormous bribes to get their kids accepted into some of America's most prestigious colleges and universities in what would come to be called the "Varsity Blues" scandal. When the news broke, many people called me to ask if any of the families we work with had been caught up in the scandal. For me, that was an amusing question, because when families initially call me to discuss possibly working with my team, one of the first things I say to them is "Understand that your kid is going to work *hard* in our program." No one who finds that pitch compelling is going to pay tens of thousands of dollars to have someone take the ACT exam for their kid.

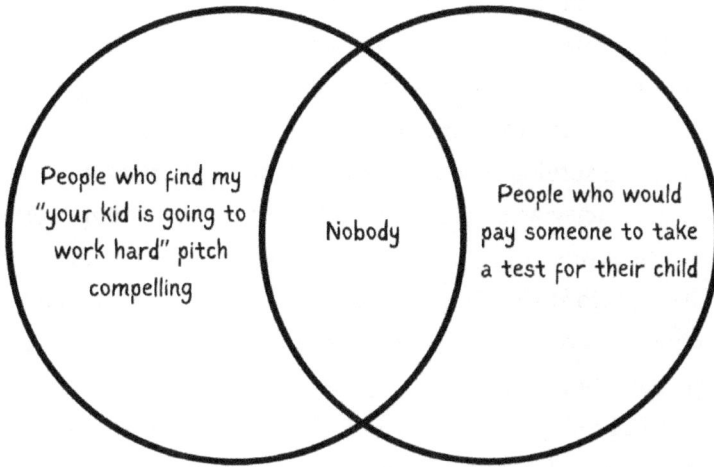

A Venn diagram with two overlapping circles. The left circle is labeled "People who find my "your kid is going to work hard" pitch compelling". The right circle is labeled "People who would pay someone to take a test for their child". The overlapping region is labeled "Nobody".

Nevertheless, it's worth taking a moment to discuss why so many people *did* get caught up in the scandal. I've been helping students navigate the college admissions process for over 20 years now, and I've watched as the job market has become more global, with top companies shifting more work abroad, where potential employees may well have received a better math and science education than students get here in the U.S. In the last couple years, I've seen automation driven by AI begin eliminating entry-level work. For families already in the upper levels of society socioeconomically, all of whom hope to ensure that their kids have at least a similar lifestyle, these forces have converged to produce a feeling that the most likely way to achieve that goal is to get their kids into a handful of blue-chip companies (legacy brands like Procter & Gamble, Disney, or Nike) or industries (like high tech, consulting, or finance).

But as more entry-level work goes overseas or is consumed by automation, the number of jobs in these blue-chip companies and industries for students right out of college is small enough that they increasingly hire from just a handful of elite colleges and universities, principally the "Ivy plus" schools (the Ivy League schools plus a handful of other elite universities, such as Stanford, MIT, Duke, and Northwestern). This is one force increasing the pressure on higher-income families to get their kids into these schools.

Another force is the sheer ease of applying these days. I'm old enough to have applied to colleges by threading paper applications into a typewriter. That kind of process created a non-monetary cost to applying, just because of the amount of work it took to submit an application. With the rise of online applications, and services such as the Common App, applying to one more school can be as easy as clicking a couple buttons. Now elite colleges are awash in applications, and admissions rates at top schools have dropped to single digits: Stanford and Harvard have dropped below 4%, Pomona College (my alma mater) is down to 7%, and even UC Berkeley, which in the 1990s still had an acceptance rate close to 30%, is down to 11%. I only applied to four colleges, but today's students routinely apply to 12—15 schools, and it's not at all uncommon for students to apply to more than 20. These numbers drive down admissions rates, which therefore creates additional pressure.

A third force is the increasing pressure on elite colleges and universities to diversify, both racially and socioeconomically. Socioeconomic diversification is straightforwardly good for society overall, but socioeconomic diversity has the practical effect of reducing the number of spots available in elite colleges for the children of higher-income families.

If you're wondering why I've focused on children from higher-income families in the last few paragraphs, it's because I want you to understand why so many families might find the "Varsity Blues" scam appealing. Put all three of the forces above together, and you have a pressure cooker of cutthroat competition that higher-income kids are thrown into. I once worked with a 5th-grader over the summer preparing her to take the SSAT, a standardized test that is used in the admission process for private middle schools. Her father said to me at the start, "Look, 99th percentile scores on all three sections is the goal." When I asked why he was so insistent on such a maximally aggressive score goal, he said, "We're Asian. The expectation is that we have scores like this. If the scores aren't perfect, or at least near-perfect, we're cooked in the application process."

So, despite my repeated caveat that there's no way I can guarantee scores like that, he had me work with his daughter. In each of our first few lessons, she arrived having completed none of the homework I'd given her, so when

I sat her down to give her The Talk about getting her homework done, she said, "I don't have time to do your homework."

That was a surprising response, and when I said, "Um, you're 11, how do you not have time for my homework?" she responded, "Let me tell you how! When this lesson is done I'll head over for a two-hour squash workout, and then from there to two hours of 'Russian math,' and then from there to a voice lesson, and then from there I'll eat a little food in the car on my way to another squash workout, and then from there I'll go to my writing tutor, and then I'll get home around 10 PM, look at your homework sitting on my desk, ignore it, and pass out."

By the time she was done explaining her schedule, *I* was tired. So I made her a deal: if she would let me push her as hard as I could in our lessons, I would not give her homework anymore. That's what we did, and when she took the SSAT that fall, she actually *did* score 99th percentile on all three sections.

That story gives a sense of what so many higher-income kids go through on the road to elite college admissions. Their parents are already planning for it in middle school, putting together the years of extracurriculars, getting extra academic opportunities (in fact, many of them will come to me and my team for enrichment their schools cannot provide), and in general building the resumes that they know colleges will want to see from them. I'm not suggesting you feel sorry for these kids, *per se*, but growing up in a low-income neighborhood, I just always assumed that kids from the higher-income levels in society were all spoiled and lazy, and... that's just not true. In fact, virtually all of them are incredibly hardworking kids who will spend up to a decade of their young lives doing some version of the academic and extracurricular grind that my SSAT student described, all to gain a little bit of an edge in a cutthroat, black-box college admissions process.

That's why, when the "Varsity Blues" guy came along, singing his siren song of a "side door" that could guarantee elite college admission without all that grinding, some people allowed themselves to be seduced by it. Again, I'm not suggesting you should feel sorry for any of them; they all made unambiguously terrible ethical decisions in participating in his scheme. Rather, I'm suggesting that these folks are the canary in the coal mine, sending you an important signal of what elite college admissions has become in this country.

That's how the process affects higher-income kids; how does the process affect lower-income kids? After all, they can't be expected to have lots of fancy extracurriculars or academic opportunities outside of school. It's effectively impossible for them to meet the same bar as the higher income kids, so elite colleges, under cultural pressure to diversify both racially and socioeconomically, have had to devise alternate pathways. For a long time, race was one of those alternate pathways, but the Supreme Court ruled out race as an explicit tool in 2023. Now, applications have questions inviting students to discuss an "identity" they have or a "hardship" they've overcome, essentially inviting kids to self-exploit their demographics or the adversity they've faced in life. The unspoken logic of it is that if there's one thing lower income kids can outcompete higher income kids in, it's in their demographics and in the amount of adversity they've had to face. But I'd invite you, dear reader, to ponder whether aggressive self-exploitation is really the best way to help lower income kids compete.

Here's a different way: when I joined Advantage Testing in 2003, in our New York City office, I learned about a partnership we had with Prep for Prep,[82] a private program which identifies high academic potential, ethnic minority kids in the public middle school system. The program invests in developing them in middle school, and then it pays for them to attend New York City's private high schools. The kids are forged in what are mostly pretty challenging public school environments, and when they are transplanted into a private high school, where they no longer have to fight against the headwinds of the environment around them, they almost inevitably become extraordinarily successful.

When they are old enough, Advantage Testing provides standardized test prep to the students, and the students all go on to score extremely well. At the Prep for Prep graduation ceremony each year, each student walks across

---

[82] The chapter QR will take you to the Prep for Prep website. It's an organization that has done amazing work, and I'd encourage you to check it out.

the stage, and the college they will be attending in the fall is announced. That list is basically a parade of Ivy plus names; since the Prep for Prep kids have the private school pedigree, the great grades and test scores, and racial/socioeconomic diversity, they crush the college application process.

But in the end, the program uses race as a primary criterion, and so in 2003, twenty years before the Supreme Court would issue its ruling disallowing the use of race in admissions, Advantage Testing joined members of the Prep for Prep board and others to launch a new organization, Leadership Enterprise for a Diverse America (LEDA),[83] a program that would use socioeconomics, not race, as its primary screening tool.

LEDA identifies low-income, high-potential kids in high schools that have no history of sending students to Ivy plus colleges, and it brings them to Princeton's campus over the summer between their junior and senior year in high school. There, they get academic enrichment, college counseling, and standardized test preparation. We at Advantage Testing provide the test preparation; I taught some of those classes in the first few years, before I moved to California to found Advantage Testing there. The program is wildly successful; the students have an average family income of just over $30,000, and of the most recent cohort of 100 students, 56 were admitted to an Ivy League school, Stanford, or MIT, and 96 of them were admitted to at least one top-60 school.

Thus, we see that given access to the same kind of academic, test prep, and college counseling resources, lower income kids are perfectly capable of competing with higher income kids. But since they don't have access to those resources, the college admissions process turns into the two-track process we've discussed: one track for higher income kids to run themselves ragged for a decade in the focused pursuit of every possible edge in the admissions game, and a second track for lower income kids to try and get close enough to the higher income kids that self-exploiting their circumstances can bridge the gap and get them a coveted admission.

---

[83] The chapter QR will take you to LEDA's website. It's a great organization, and I encourage you to read about them. I've always enjoyed teaching LEDA scholars!

That's our current process for admission to selective colleges and universities. Does it sound... not great to you? My team and I have helped thousands of kids over the last couple decades master the process and get that coveted admission to an Ivy plus school, and the process sounds not great to me. So how could we improve things for all students?

Before we dive into a specific proposal, we need to have some Real Talk. As of this writing, our country is witnessing some extremely caustic battles between a handful of elite colleges and the Trump administration. The Trump administration is trying to solve, in its own articulation, problems it perceives around speech, potential discrimination against Whites and Asians in admissions, and suppression of conservative voices. You may or may not agree that these are problems; roughly half the country seems to fall on each side of that question.

Our discussion here, though, is completely different. The problem we are trying to solve is an out-of-control admissions process that manages to treat high- and low-income students differentially, yet equally badly. But that process applies to only a handful of the most selective colleges and universities, which means the focus of the proposal below is necessarily on those schools, the same set of schools that the Trump administration has focused on. It would be easy, given that overlap, to conflate what we're talking about with what the Trump administration is doing, and there will very likely be people who will deliberately conflate them for their own cynical reasons. But that's a mistake: the proposal below solves a real problem in a way that offers latitude to the schools it would apply to.

Here's my proposal, a proposal which would require action at the federal level. But given that California has the largest public school system in America, and some of the best colleges and universities in the country, the leadership of the California Department of Education could demonstrate needed initiative in advocating for this proposal, or something broadly similar.

Under this proposal, every college that accepts fewer than half its applicants would choose one of the following three options:

- **Option 1:** Prior to accepting applications in an admissions cycle, the college would have to publicly announce a set of objective criteria that would constitute the bar that the college believes a successful applicant should meet. At the application deadline, every applicant who has met the bar would be placed in a pool, and the first 90% of seats would be awarded by lottery to students in the pool. The remaining 10% of the seats the college would be allowed to auction off, but only to the remaining applicants in the pool.
- **Option 2:** Continue using whatever admissions process you use today! But you must expand the size of your first-year class by 10% every five years in order to be allowed to continue using without consequence whatever admissions process you use today.
- **Option 3:** Continue using whatever admissions process you use today! But then we revoke your nonprofit status, until such a time as you switch to either Option 1 or Option 2.

Why you should like option 1: In this option, every student who meets the bar has an equal chance at admission, regardless of family income, race, gender, choice of major, etc. And remember—a college can set the bar wherever they want! Harvard can feel free to set their bar really high. But anyone who clears that bar has an equal chance: gone are the days of "We need higher test scores because we're Asian." Gone are the days of "We need to stretch our kid with activities until they're right on the edge of anxiety and depression just to try and get an extra edge."

As for the auction piece, you might be thinking, "Gee, doesn't that mean wealthier people have an advantage?" If that's what you're thinking, I've got bad news for you: wealthier people having an advantage is *how the system works today.* It's not spoken about much because in practice the higher income kids pay more, and the extra money turns into the financial aid that allows lower income students to attend. Put another way, the higher-income kids subsidize the lower-income kids. My proposal simply streamlines that process and moves it out into the open. By the way, if you're reading this and are in the top 1–2% of the income spectrum, good news: no more multiyear shadow "development" dance with your target college. Just make your bid if you don't get accepted through the lottery.

Thus, my proposal is substantially fairer than the current process, and it involves less torturing kids for years before throwing them into an arbitrary, black-box admissions process, which is what we do today.

Why you should like option 2: The behavior of elite colleges and universities is functionally indistinguishable from classic cartel behavior in that the market demand for the product is extraordinarily high, yet the producers of the product make no effort to expand their supply. This option fixes that by mandating that if the schools are not going to choose a neutral admissions process like that outlined in option 1, then they have to expand the supply of their level of education by increasing the number of slots available. The schools have already clearly demonstrated that they will not do this in the absence of external pressure.

Personally, I would like to see all selective colleges and universities choose either option 1 or option 2. But let's also talk briefly about:

Why you should like option 3: Harvard is currently tax exempt. That means you, dear reader, currently subsidize Harvard's arbitrary, black-box admissions process. Your tax dollars subsidize an institution that as of today is sitting on an endowment whose value is over *fifty billion dollars*. Philosophically, I believe that in a free society, Harvard is entitled to have whatever admissions process they want. But they are *not* entitled to taxpayer support for that process. If Harvard wants taxpayer support, then they can either make their admissions process more fair and transparent, or they can expand their size to serve more students.

This three-option proposal allows every selective college to make their choice about what's more important to them: run a fair, transparent admissions process, serve more students, or pay taxes like everybody else. The choice would be theirs. Note also that this policy change would solve some of the problems the Trump administration is trying to solve, but in a much less onerous manner: no multimillion dollar payouts, no intrusive demands for sensitive internal admissions data, and so forth.

A final note: remember, this process would only apply to colleges that accept fewer than half their applicants. It wouldn't affect community colleges at all, for instance, since they typically accept the vast majority of their applicants. Though this change would require federal action, the California Department of Education could use its bully pulpit to advocate for such a solution, and the Department should do so since it would level the playing field and expand access for students of all backgrounds. Of course, this requires a type of leadership that we have never had at the Department, and so we as voters have to choose that leadership if we want to make change happen.

How You Can Help

There are lots of ways you can get involved in the issue of improving access to higher education:

Basic level:

Leadership for a Diverse America (LEDA) and organizations like it (Mission Graduates, Peninsula Bridge, Questbridge, the Jack Kent Cooke Foundation) that identify and help talented students based on income level each have a newsletter that you can sign up for online. Sign up for a newsletter, and when good news comes out, share it on your social media and mention that you support the organization's work. The chapter QR will take you to links to these organizations' websites, and if you know of other, similar organizations, send them to me at gus@AisforAvg.com.

Volunteer with a local nonprofit that does work in this space. Depending on the organization, there could be opportunities to help with academic work, test prep, applications, and shorter- or longer-term mentoring. For example, my team teaches a pro bono ACT class for Mission Graduates[84] in

---

[84] The chapter QR has a link to Mission Graduates. I encourage you to check them out; they do great work in San Francisco.

San Francisco. I taught that class myself for many years, and I can tell you that it's very rewarding work.

Intermediate level:

Coordinate with a local under-resourced school to bring in some people who came from similar low-income backgrounds and went on to selective colleges and successful careers to speak at the school about how they did it and what the challenges were along the way. Kids are most likely to respond to such stories when they see people like themselves telling them. Use your professional network to source possible speakers, and raise funds if necessary to bring the speakers to the school.

Work with a local university to establish a program that assists low-income students in your local community in applying to selective colleges and universities. For example, my team works with Tulane University's Louisiana Center for College Access.[85] Tulane leverages their connections in the wider community to identify students for the program, and we provide at-cost ACT tutoring for the students. See if a college or university in your area has a similar program; if so, volunteer with it. If not, consider partnering with them to create a similar program.

Jedi Level:

Establish a nonprofit that assists low-income students in your local community in applying to selective colleges and universities. There are many forms this assistance can take: assisting with the college admissions process, including test prep or essay writing assistance, for example. Or you can raise funds for one or more scholarships for local low-income students. Or you can organize mentoring for such students, who often need various kinds of support to make it through college and the initial job search that comes after. These efforts vary in the amount of financial backing and volunteer

---

[85] The chapter QR has a link to the Louisiana Center for College Access. Check them out!

support they require, but find the combination that fits with your skills and your community's needs and make it happen.

It will take a lot of work sustained over several years to establish a self-sustaining nonprofit operation, but you're a Jedi. If anyone can make it happen, you can!

* * *

Chapter 18 QR code

Technical and professional education shall be made generally available and higher education shall be equally accessible to all on the basis of merit.
- Article 26, Universal Declaration of Human Rights

VII

How do we make change happen?

19

Interlude: The Artful Slacker

When I hire tutors, one thing I look for is the ability to work with a wide range of personalities. Each kid who comes to us is different from the others, and so it's not useful to have someone on the team who can really only work well with one type of personality.

That said, each of us has a personality type that is our wheelhouse, a personality type that we have an unusually easy time building a strong relationship with. When the bond is that easy and that strong between the tutor and the student, the results are almost invariably a home run. For me, that personality type is the Artful Slacker.

You probably know an Artful Slacker. They are very obviously quite smart, but they are entirely unimpressed by authority. Give them a task or a topic that they are interested in, and they will perform that task or talk about that topic quickly, easily, and well. Give them a task or a topic that they are NOT interested in, and they will engage in a spirited, and oftentimes quite creative, campaign of active and passive resistance. Consequently, Artful Slackers tend to have a long history of underperforming their considerable potential, at least when it comes to school.

Artful Slackers are my people.

Thus, when "Spike" first came to see me, we hit it off right away. Spike was a classic Artful Slacker: super smart, naturally curious, verbally fluent far beyond his fifteen years, and wholly uninterested in mundane matters like "SAT prep" or "math homework." I knew I had my hands full with him.

In my experience, the best strategy with the Artful Slacker is to let them be themselves. I let Spike be Spike. As I said, he was naturally curious and had a wide-ranging mind, and when he wanted to talk about whatever was on his mind in the moment, I gave him pretty broad latitude to do so. An outside observer tasked with measuring how much of our lessons covered SAT prep and math instruction would probably have reported that two-thirds of our time was wasted. But that's not true: by letting Spike be Spike, he came to enjoy our lessons, and given his level of intellect, with a happy Spike I could accomplish what I needed to accomplish in one-third of the time. Did I always have a happy Spike? Of course not. He was a teenage boy, after all. Let me tell you a quick story to illustrate that.

I have a thing I do for my friend group called "Overheard in today's lesson," in which I relay funny conversations I have with my students. Spike made the "Overheard" series many, many times, but here is one of my favorites. By the time of this conversation, Spike had already crushed the SAT, gotten good grades in math, and gotten accepted to an Ivy League school. At that point, I was helping him with his college calculus class...

(8/22/12) Overheard in today's lesson:

Gus: "What y-value will it take to make this function continuous?"

Spike: "I dunno man."

Gus: "There's a hole in this graph at $x = 3$. What y-value would plug the hole?"

Spike: "I dunno man."

Gus: "Well, you take this x-value and plug- ... Spike? SPIKE!"

Spike: "What?"

Gus: "Pay attention!"

Spike: "Dude, this stuff is too hard. I'm like France in World War II- I've already given up."

Gus: [eyeroll]

Spike: "Seriously, it's already over, and now I'm just collaborating. I'm collaborating with the part of my mind that says this is too hard. Your math has totally blitzkrieged me into submission."

Though tutoring Spike was not easy, it was certainly very entertaining, and in the end I helped Spike successfully navigate calculus. I had dinner with him not so long ago; he's in his thirties, married now, with a successful career on the business side of tech. He took a while to really find his way, but he did, as the vast majority of kids will do, if you give them space to do it.

There's a lesson in this story about how we should think about schooling. I was successful with Spike because I let him be himself. I think we should let kids be kids. I'm pretty confident that it's accurate to say that parenting styles have drifted away from that, and I'm 100% confident that *schooling* has drifted away from that. I think if we gave kids more time to play and just be kids (taking their phones away while they do it), it would benefit them in two ways. One, it would make them happier; i.e., it would help their mental health. And two, it would leave them better able to learn during actual instructional time. But the trend in schooling is the other way: chain the kids to desks for ever longer periods of time. If you're wondering why we have an "anxious generation," I'd assert that's part of the reason.

20

The Superintendent of Public Instruction

Where there is no vision, the people perish.
- Proverbs 29:18

* * *

In this book, we've examined reforms that could be implemented at every level: local, district-level pilot projects, systemwide reforms at the state level, and even a proposal for the federal level. How do we get any of these ideas implemented? How do we overcome the incredible resistance to change that politics imposes on the school system?

Ladies and gentlemen, please allow me to introduce the strongest individual lever for change that exists in the school system, a lever for change that California has never used: the Superintendent of Public Instruction. The Superintendent is a constitutionally created office that manages the K–12 public education system at the statewide level. And although in most states the Superintendent is an appointed position, in California it's an *elected* position, which means the Superintendent has some latitude to operate independently from the Governor, the legislature, and the State Board of Education (whose members are picked by the Governor.)

Given that latitude, the Superintendent's role can be properly thought of as having three separate dimensions: an administrator, a facilitator, and an advocate. Let's examine each of these dimensions.

Dimension 1: The Administrator

The position of the Superintendent was created to be the chief administrator of the public school system statewide. The system is designed by the legislature and the Governor via the State Board of Education, but it is administered by the Superintendent. Thus, the Superintendent cannot unilaterally make statewide changes to the design of the public school system; that requires persuading some subset of the legislature, the Governor, and the State Board. But the Superintendent does have some real power to decide the structure, priorities, and processes of the California Department of Education (CDE), and because of that, there are some opportunities for change within the CDE that the Superintendent could drive.

The CDE serves as an interface between the legislature, governor, and state board of education on the one hand, and the individual school districts and county boards of education on the other. Today, the CDE's functions are focused primarily on compliance requirements rather than focused on the question, "What can this department be doing to make it easier for schools to educate kids, even as we satisfy whatever compliance requirements the state and federal governments impose?" That's a subtle but very important difference that significantly impacts how individual school districts interact with the state.

As an example of that impact, here in the Bay Area, the Ravenswood school district, which educates a large population of low-income kids from the East Palo Alto area, employs several people full-time just to deal with compliance tasks imposed by the state through the CDE. Each of those full-time people makes well over $100,000 in salary and benefits, so Ravenswood is forced to spend approximately *half a million* taxpayer dollars each year just on bureaucratic compliance. That's half a million dollars that aren't paying for more reading specialists, or more science equipment for the lab, or more art classes. And therein lies an opportunity: a Superintendent with a change mindset could form a working group composed of people from the CDE, from county boards of education, and from individual school districts and charge them with identifying all the current compliance processes and then designing a new set of processes that satisfy all the compliance obligations imposed by the state and the federal government but that take only half the time and resources to complete. If the working group can design such a process, then the CDE should implement it. Cutting compliance time in half would free up hundreds of thousands of dollars in administrative staff costs in a district like Ravenswood, and those resources could then be repurposed to actually teaching kids, and all *without raising taxes*.

Similarly, the Superintendent could form a parallel working group whose task would be to analyze the org chart for the CDE and determine if there is a better way to organize the department to make it easier and more helpful for districts and county boards to deal with. Together with the working group, the Superintendent could devise and implement a new org chart and thus make the CDE a more efficient and much more supportive organization for our school districts and county boards of education. Again, this is something that could be accomplished without raising taxes.

Such process and organizational redesign efforts rarely happen in political organizations because the work involved is long, tedious, and extremely unsexy. Process and organizational design are almost lethally boring to regular folks, which means the media will pay little attention, and the legislature will be at best indifferent and at worst actively hostile to the effort. It would take probably a year to identify who would be the most productive people to put on the working groups, another year for them to produce recommendations, and then another 1–2 years for the Superintendent to implement the recommendations. That's an entire term of the Superintendent, all to accomplish some things that the Superintendent would never be rewarded for politically, and that the public would almost certainly never notice. And yet, the work has to get done anyway, because it would make a real difference, and it could be accomplished without solving the immense political problem of changing the behavior of the legislature and the governor.

That's a lot of work just as an administrator. But that work merely scratches the surface. Let's talk about:

Dimension 2: The Facilitator

We discussed examples of pilot projects in areas like reading and math that could be run at the district level with the support of district-level Superintendents who were open to experimentation and innovation. However, it takes active, supportive leadership at the top, at the CDE, to identify and bring together such local-level Superintendents. Furthermore, to avoid the political constraint of the legislature, funding for the pilots would have to be sourced from the private and nonprofit sectors, and the Superintendent of Public Instruction, as the second-largest megaphone for education after the Secretary of Education in Washington DC, is best equipped to lead the effort to source the funding.

With bold leadership, the Superintendent of Public Instruction can create a culture of experimentation and innovation, and by driving initiatives at the district level, they can create *pockets* of change within the system, and do so without being constrained by the legislature, the State Board, or the Governor. By insisting that all experimental initiatives be data-driven and rigorously analyzed, over time successful projects could be highlighted and examined for scalability and potential rollout to other districts, and perhaps the entire system. That brings us to the third dimension:

Dimension 3: The Advocate

For better or for worse, our school system is designed by the state legislature and the Governor, via the State Board of Education. Put another way, the system is designed by politicians, and as politicians they will respond consistently to one thing and one thing only: political pressure. Thus, a vital role of the Superintendent of Public Instruction is to do the hard, painstaking work of helping organize grassroots interest in the school system, and then to become the mechanism that transforms that interest into political pressure and focuses that political pressure on Sacramento. Then and only then will we be able to drive the necessary changes to the system to ensure that every child in California gets a decent education.

Thus, we can see that the role of the Superintendent of Public Instruction is truly three-dimensional, and with the right person, the office could be an active, supportive partner to our individual school districts and an energetic, powerful force for positive change in our school system. When I showed an early draft of this point to a friend who had spent his entire career in the California public school system, he exclaimed, "This is ridiculous! None of this will ever happen. That's not how the Superintendent's office works!"

One of my favorite movies of all time is *The Princess Bride.* In it, there is a scene in which Wesley and the Princess Buttercup must enter the Fire Swamp, and as they run in, Buttercup says, "We'll never survive!" and Wesley responds, "Nonsense! You're only saying that because no one ever has." My friend is correct that the Superintendent's office does not today work the way I described above, and it hasn't worked that way in at least a couple generations. But that's not because of the laws of nature. It's not even because of the laws of men. It's simply a *choice.* It's been the choice of the last several inhabitants of the office to simply be one-dimensional Administrators, attending the monthly Board meetings, giving pretty speeches about equity, collecting a $200,000 per year paycheck, and otherwise doing nothing.

But the great beauty of democracy is that no matter what has happened in the past, We the People can always start making different choices. The Superintendent of Public Instruction is an elected office, and in 2026 we'll have our next opportunity to make a different choice as voters. When that time comes, it's important that we choose someone who will view the job three-dimensionally and be a true force for change in our schools. That's the best choice for our kids, and I hope you'll join me in making it.

A leader takes people where they want to go.
A great leader takes people where they don't necessarily want to go,
but ought to be.
– Rosalynn Carter

VIII

How can you help?

21

Conclusion

The most common way people give up their power is by thinking
they don't have any.
- Alice Walker

* * *

If you've made it this far, you've already read many, many different ways that *you* can help. But the most powerful, profound things you can do to help are here, at the end of the book.

Basic level:

The most basic, and yet the most important of all things, is ***vote***.

I understand that the politics of our age may be very disheartening for you. I understand that you may feel that your vote doesn't matter. I understand that you may feel that nothing will ever change. And I'm not really trying to change your mind about any of that, *per se*. Instead, I'm asking you to consider this: in 2018, which was the last time the Superintendent's seat was open, a total of $61 million dollars were spent on that race.[86] Sixty-one *million* dollars. For an office that most people don't even know exists! That kind of spending wouldn't happen unless the office were truly *important*. I'm not trying to change your mind about anything, but I am asking you to consider all that you've read in this book that we could be doing differently to help our kids, if we had the right person in office. I'm not trying to change your mind about our political process broadly, but I'm asking you to consider that if you actually have read this far, then you understand on a gut level how important education is for our kids, and how important it is that we fix our schools.

I'm not here to change your mind about our electoral process. I'm here to ask you, as a personal favor to me, given all that we've been through together over these many pages, to fill in one bubble on your ballot. And if that's the only bubble you fill out, that's okay! You don't have to fill out any other races; you're allowed to vote only for that race, if you want. Please understand that I'm not *recommending* that you do that; it really is better if you vote in the other races on your ballot too. If you're looking for recommendations on whom to vote for, hit me up at gus@aisforavg.com and I'll put you on my mailing list. I'll send out recommendations when the time comes.

But if you only have energy to fill out one bubble, let it be the bubble for Superintendent of Public Instruction. I promise you'll have done something meaningful!

Intermediate level:

Elections are most likely to produce change candidates when people who don't normally vote actually come out and vote. Be the person who helps get them in the game!

Assign yourself as homework to identify at least three people in your life, whom you know reasonably well and have a strong relationship with, and

---

[86] The chapter QR will take you to a link to a *CalMatters* article that quotes and sources this figure.

whom you know probably don't vote. Play a long game: don't try to get them to do something the very first time you talk to them. Get there in stages over several interactions with them: plant a seed by mentioning that you read this book and found it compelling, and then give a few reasons why. Then at another time, mention whom you have decided is compelling and give some reasons why. Do that on a couple of different occasions, making sure to mention the name of the person you've decided to support (getting the person to recognize the name is key!), but don't be in a hurry to make your ask yet. If you are patient, over time you'll get some green shoots from the seeds you've planted.

When the ballots finally go out, then it's your time to shine. Harvest the votes you've been cultivating by saying that this election means a lot to you, and you're asking that as a favor to you, they vote for your preferred candidate. Don't be surprised if they aren't receptive to that at first; most people who don't vote choose not to vote because they've lost all faith in our democratic system, and it's important to respect that point of view because the reasons behind it are real. Tell them you respect where they're coming from, and you aren't trying to change their mind about any of that, but that you're still asking that as a favor to you, they bubble in just one bubble for your candidate. Remind them that it's totally fine to only fill out that one race if they want. Then say you understand if they don't, but you'll be deeply grateful if they do. And leave it at that.

If you get half the people you cultivated to go along, then honestly, you've done great work! Seriously. This kind of work is *hard*. But it is powerful, and it is meaningful. And it's how we actually make changes in our society.

If you still have more energy, get involved in one of your local school board races. Find a candidate whose values are in alignment with what you found compelling in this book, and volunteer for their campaign. Campaigns never have enough volunteers, and local school board races are generally small enough that if you put enough people together, your team can have at least one conversation with a sizable fraction of the people who will vote in the election. People talking with people: that is American democracy at its best. And though you of course will not agree with everyone you talk to, you will find, if you keep at it, that the process will remind you of a very important truth: that the vast majority of people are fundamentally good and want very much to do the right thing. It will be, to quote a book from another century, chicken soup for your soul.

Jedi level

If you truly feel the call to leadership, then get in the game and run for your local school board.

We live in a very fraught time when it comes to politics, and it is not a game for the faint of heart. But the primary qualification you need to have to be successful in politics is simply the willingness to take a chance and run. You'll need to prepare properly for it; do the exercises in this book that involve getting to know your district: the demographics of it, the finances of it, the people already on the board, etc. Attend the meetings for a while so you can see what the issues are and who the personalities are. See if you can connect with someone who has won a school board or other local elected office in your area and get their advice and perspective. But when you're ready, jump in! America needs more engaged citizens to get involved in the political process, and it's a profoundly meaningful thing to do.

I can tell you from experience that politics is really hard, and it takes strength of will, strength of character, the humility to learn from others and from your own mistakes, and the inner steel to survive the inevitable attacks you'll take from whoever your opponent is. In short, it takes a Jedi mindset. And while I obviously cannot guarantee that you will win your race, I *can* guarantee that you won't regret taking the chance. It's one of the bravest, most quintessentially *American* things you can do.

Are you a Jedi? Then get in the game! I'd love to see you in it.

* * *

Chapter 21 QR code

To give the victory to the right, not bloody bullets,
but peaceful ballots only, are necessary.
– Abraham Lincoln

Afterword

But I don't live in California. How much of this stuff applies to me?

* * *

California is my adopted home; I waited a long time in life to live in a quiet little house with an ocean view. So in writing this book, I decided to focus specifically on California's schools. But the short answer to the question, "How much of this applies to me if I don't live in California?" is, "most of it, actually!"

First, the focus of this book, which is on the problem of the two-tiered outcome gap between Whites and Asians on the one hand, and Blacks and Latinos and Native Americans on the other, is a focus that belongs in every state. I am not aware of any state that does not face the problem of a two-tiered outcome to some degree. No matter where you live, this is a problem you can work on.

Second, I made the case that the most powerful lever you can pull to create momentum for change is an elected Superintendent, since that person will be independent of the state legislature and the governor and therefore does not face the same political constraints. Unfortunately, only a few other states have elected Superintendents. As of this writing, that list appears to be:

- Arizona
- Georgia
- Idaho
- Montana
- North Carolina

- North Dakota
- Oklahoma
- South Carolina
- Washington
- Wisconsin
- Wyoming

For everyone else, your Superintendent or equivalent is appointed by your governor or your State Board of Education. *Ballotpedia* has a good summary of how the Superintendent is chosen in each state.[87] For those lucky enough to live in one of the states listed above, you can focus your efforts on getting someone good into this one office, and then that person can pursue the same kind of three-dimensional approach I outlined in the conclusion.

In every other state, getting a good Superintendent means pressuring either the governor or the state legislature, depending on which one is the one that chooses the Superintendent. No matter which one you need to pressure, it's a tall order, because a million other interest groups will be pressuring them too. In your case, you're probably better off focusing on the grassroots level: you can focus on getting a good Superintendent for your local district, and then support that person's efforts to drive change in your district and to seek out likeminded peers in other districts. Note: if that person does indeed drive some change in your district, that change will almost inevitably ruffle feathers, and so if you feel the person is making a good faith effort to bring needed change, you'll need to be ready to protect them politically by turning out support when it's reelection time. The people whose feathers got ruffled will certainly turn out, so you and your people will need to be ready to go.

Beyond working on the electoral side of the issue, remember that we discussed many ways you could get involved directly in education by working with local nonprofits or by working with your local business leadership, which often is very receptive to getting involved with schools if there is some organized way for them to do so. If you think you have a good education

---

[87] The afterword QR will take you to the *Ballotpedia* link.

nonprofit like Cabrillo Education Foundation or a good business group that's interested in education, like Nosterra, then send their website to me at gus@aisforavg.com and I'll start compiling them on my website to make the search easier for the next person from your state. You of course should also consider being part of a group that carefully monitors your local and state school boards, to make sure they don't slip any misguided *A is for Average* policies by you unnoticed, as they tried to do in San Francisco.

Remember that there are basic, intermediate, and Jedi level ways to get involved, so you can find the right level of engagement for you. What matters most is that you get involved in *some* way, whatever that way is. Remember: our American lifestyle and our children's future depend on our getting education right, so everything you do to help move the ball down the field is important and meaningful.

Seek out the Jedi among you, or better yet be a Jedi yourself! Either way, there's no need to be in this fight alone. Find likeminded people, speak out against the *A is for Average* mentality wherever you find it, support the people who are driving change in your state, and in time, we will see all across our country that our schools have become the engines of uplift that they have the capacity to be.

There's a lot of work to do, and a long road ahead, but I'm glad to be in this fight with you!

* * *

Afterword QR code

Knowledge will forever govern ignorance; and a people who mean to be their own governors must arm themselves with the power which knowledge gives.

— James Madison

Acknowledgments

It is a truth universally acknowledged that writing a book is a real pain in the butt. And as someone who has tutored hundreds of students in writing, I have always expounded with passionate intensity that the essence of writing is re-writing.

Yet somehow, I didn't think any of that would apply to *me*. I thought I would just quickly download a lifetime of thoughts about education directly into a tightly structured, coherent, *pretty awesome* book. Then I would show that to some people who would all agree it was *pretty awesome*, then do some light editing and ship it off to print—easy-peasy, lemon-squeezy. It was really a wonderful dream.

Unfortunately, that dream ended up bearing no resemblance to reality. Thus, the first people I want to acknowledge are the people who read the first draft of this book, a draft that could only be described as "dreadful." Each of them contributed important thoughts to the development of the final product: Joel Aufrecht (introduction), Laszlo Bock (how you can help), Gerri Bock (higher education), Lance Christensen (school choice), Tim Dec (preface), Matt Demmer (the Superintendent), Gregg Dieguez (*everything needs more evidence!*), Rick Giorgetti (math), Bill Jackson (structure and presentation), Lillian Oliveri (interlude stories), Sean McPhetridge (school funding), Jonathan Myers (narrative elements), Will Sherman (reading), Luke Taylor (interlude stories), Mark Wyland (career technical education), and Luke Youngvorst (the subtitle). Lance's feedback led me to Len Gilroy and Zachary Christensen at the Reason Foundation, and discussions with them led to the piece on teacher retirement reform. Paul Bock challenged me to make the case for why we should even have public education at all, and making that case is important.

No one person could ever solve California's education crisis, and no one person could ever view policy from every perspective necessary. Thus, I am grateful to those whose extensive backgrounds in education policy helped pressure-test the ideas in this book: Lance Christensen, Sean McPhetridge, Mark Wyland, Virginia "Vickie" Morales, Charlotte Hu, and Catherine Watson-Short. Santina "Sandy" Vavrousek also gave valuable feedback from a student's perspective, which all too often is lacking in discussions about education reform.

In addition to reading the first draft, Ishaan Prasad is largely responsible for this book being published before the year 2060, which is about the pace I was on before he got involved. Georgeanna Cannon was my superb research assistant, and she saved me untold hours pulling together background information. Kevin Hoormann at Gonzo & Plaid Publishing has been part of my journey for more decades than I care to remember. My old classmate Gregg Vanourek, an accomplished author himself, gave me valuable advice on the process of writing a book. Rebecca Krouner, in addition to reading both the first *and* second drafts for copyediting, also gave me invaluable feedback about where I should soften my tone; I get pretty passionate about the ways in which we could be doing better, and sometimes that passion leaked into my writing in unhelpful ways. My colleague Alex Reisner gave valuable edits of the second draft. Sara Patterson, a friend for over thirty years, is a profoundly gifted graphic designer and designed all the cover art for the book. Asa Mathat, as gifted a photographer as you'll ever meet, took one of the few good pictures of me that have ever been taken, and I used that in the "About the Author" section.

It was at lunch with Bill Balson and Grady Means that the idea of writing this book in the first place was hatched. I wish I had written the idea down on a napkin; that would be the most quintessentially Silicon Valley thing to have done. At least half the books I read as background over the year I spent preparing to write the book were recommendations from Matt Glotzbach. Erwin Hosono helped sharpen my thinking on project-based learning. And to circle back to Laszlo Bock, it takes a special kind of best friend to endure a year's worth of conversations on these topics on our weekly walks. His mind is like an x-ray machine that identified a hundred different points of weakness in my own thinking, all of which I did my best to address.

Which reminds me: whatever weaknesses remain in this book are surely there because I willfully ignored the advice of one or more of the folks mentioned above. The fault, dear Brutus, lies not in my readers, but in me.

I must also acknowledge my colleagues at Advantage Testing. I like to say that Advantage Testing is the NBA of tutoring: only the best of the best of the best will ever make it to that level. They are the finest educators in the country, and the 22 years that I've spent learning from them have been a singular joy. I'd particularly like to highlight my leadership team: Elisa Maassen, Rebecca Krouner, Keiko Ono, and Heather Lattanzi, who make my ship run smoothly even when I have my head wrapped up in things like writing a book. I also want to thank all the students and families that have trusted me and my team to help them on their educational journeys; I've built some deep and lasting relationships with some amazing people that way. I'd also like to thank Arun Alagappan, founder of Advantage Testing, for giving me that rarest of opportunities: the opportunity to do good *and* do well.

Finally, I want to thank my parents, Michael and Mary Mattammal, who chose a much harder life for themselves in order to give a much better life to their four kids. My belief in the power of education to transform, arguably the belief that is most fundamental to who I am, comes from them. And, above all, my amazing wife Jill, the BWE (Best Wife Ever), who in addition to reading the first draft (which she did), and being a good sport about being mentioned in the book (which she was), has been a bedrock of support in everything I've tried to do in the 20 years that I've known her. She has been patient, she has been kind, and she has never asked me for anything in return, other than a weasel, a stoat, a ferret, an ermine, an otter, a bushbaby, a baby tapir, a raccoon, a porcupine, a shaggy highland cow, a minipony, a regular pony, a Clydesdale, a lemur, a giraffe, some meerkats, an owl, some ravens, a serval, a llama, an alpaca, a red panda, a "kinkajou," which I'm not convinced is even real, a panther, a cheetah, a wombat, a regular badger, a honey badger, some baby goats, a bucket of kittens, and "more dogs." I love her more than life itself.

About the Author

Gus Mattammal is the Director of Advantage Testing of Silicon Valley. Advantage Testing has been described by the New York Times as the "premier tutoring company." Gus has led the expansion of Advantage Testing's private and pro bono activity throughout the South, Midwest, and West. As a full-time educator with Advantage Testing for over 22 years, Gus has personally worked with over 1,000 students of every race and socioeconomic background and helped them achieve their academic goals and aspirations.

Gus is an elected member of the Midcoast Community Council, representing the 12,000 people who live between Half Moon Bay and Pacifica, and serves on countywide boards dealing with transportation and with tax oversight. He is also President of SHIFT-Bay Area (www.shift-ba.org), a nonpartisan policy advocacy group focused on regional issues in the Bay Area. SHIFT-Bay Area brings together people from across the entire political spectrum to promote transparent, accountable, sustainable policies in the areas of housing, infrastructure, finance, and transportation.

When not teaching kids or working on public policy, Gus enjoys reading, taking his border collie Dixie on long walks, and spending time with his amazing wife Jill, whom he hopes to one day deserve.